Cunxin Kate Fitzp
Davies Wayne Bl
on Vicki Van Hout Edo Dav
hovan Richard Bonynge Fr
yn Nevin William Barton P
Sylvie Guillem Rhoda Robe
hes Edo de Waart Sarah Bl
man Lyndon Terracini Pete
d Nick Cave Nikki Gemme
Baz Luhrmann Wendy Mar
Fergus Linehan Bill Henso
nin Tim Sharp Graeme Mu
hes Richard Tognetti Ngaiir
esley Enoch John Olsen Li
ate Mulvany Tim Minchin P

Edited by Ashleigh Wilson

TRAN
SCEND
ENCE

50 years of unforgettable moments at the Sydney Opera House

Thames
&Hudson

 5O

WELCOME

Yvonne Weldon

A Welcome to Country is varied in our traditions across this continent. It is a practice that pays respect to the ancestors, honouring everyone on, from and of this land and the waterways, and each other, for generations and generations. This is our way. It is the way it has always been.

The impacts and devastation began here. My people give respect and so we all should. Walking together in the ancestors' footsteps as one.

We gather to celebrate the fifty years of the Sydney Opera House, a modern-day icon on land originally known as Tubowgule. This area had large midden deposits and was originally a small tidal island with rocks and a small beach at the tip of the eastern arm of Sydney Cove.

These are the lands and waters of the Gadigal people of the Eora Nation. The Eora Nation's boundaries span from the Hawkesbury in the north, the Nepean in the west and the Georges River in the south. We are the world's oldest living culture, the First Nations of the continent now known as Australia.

We also celebrate our diversity within and the diversity that has joined us from many nations and countries, coming together to unite us, where we all call home. I am, you are, we are Australian.

Ngyini ngalawangun mari budjari Gadinurda. Welcome to Gadigal. From the First Nations we say: Welcome. You are welcomed.

It is an honour and a privilege to give a Welcome to Country, to acknowledge Country and the ancestors who have gone before us and sacrificed so much. I have been granted this honour many times at the Sydney Opera House, whose sails have stood strong for fifty years, as the First Peoples of this continent now known as Australia have done for more than 65,000 years, since time immemorial.

From a yarn with Germaine Greer in 2012 to a lighting of the sails with art by First Nations women on a windy autumn night in 2021, some occasions have been absorbed into my spirit. But walking on stage in 2019 for the opening night of *Man With The Iron Neck*, a profound production by Ursula Yovich, felt different.

It had to. That night was about remembering five Aboriginal girls who had died by suicide across a nine-day period. Where was the outcry? Those girls mattered then and they matter now, but it took a play like this for their voices to be widely heard.

This was a story of intergenerational trauma and heartache that continues to reverberate through people, Country and spirit. It was also about changing the cycle through talking, sharing, truth-telling, laughing, healing. About bringing light to darkness. Creating positive opportunities for everyone.

That evening, as I looked into the audience, representation mattered. This Welcome wasn't only about recognising ancestors, Country, history. It was also about speaking for a future that recognises, honours and includes us all. That's what I try to do in a Welcome. To plant a seed. To open doors. The Opera House is a stage for the stories we need to hear, and that includes facing up to some of the hard, uncomfortable truths about our world.

The Opera House brings people together. Like the tiles on the sails, we are all part of this mosaic. Imagine what we could achieve over the next fifty years through truth-telling and inclusion. Together, we can make a difference. We must.

_Yvonne Weldon is deputy chairperson of the Metropolitan Local Aboriginal Land Council, the first Aboriginal Councillor elected to the City of Sydney Council, and the author of *Sixty-Seven Days*.

I've performed with the Sydney Symphony in her cavernous Concert Hall and sung solo in the Studio, deep in her belly. And like every artist before me and since, I've been lost in the halls of her labyrinthine undercarriage, peering through miserly windows, using the Harbour Bridge as a guiding star...

_TIM MINCHIN

Part of my process, when I write, involves a daily walk. I draw inspiration from the landscape around me. And when I worked on this project, I often walked past the Opera House to envisage my home in that building.

_WILLIAM BARTON

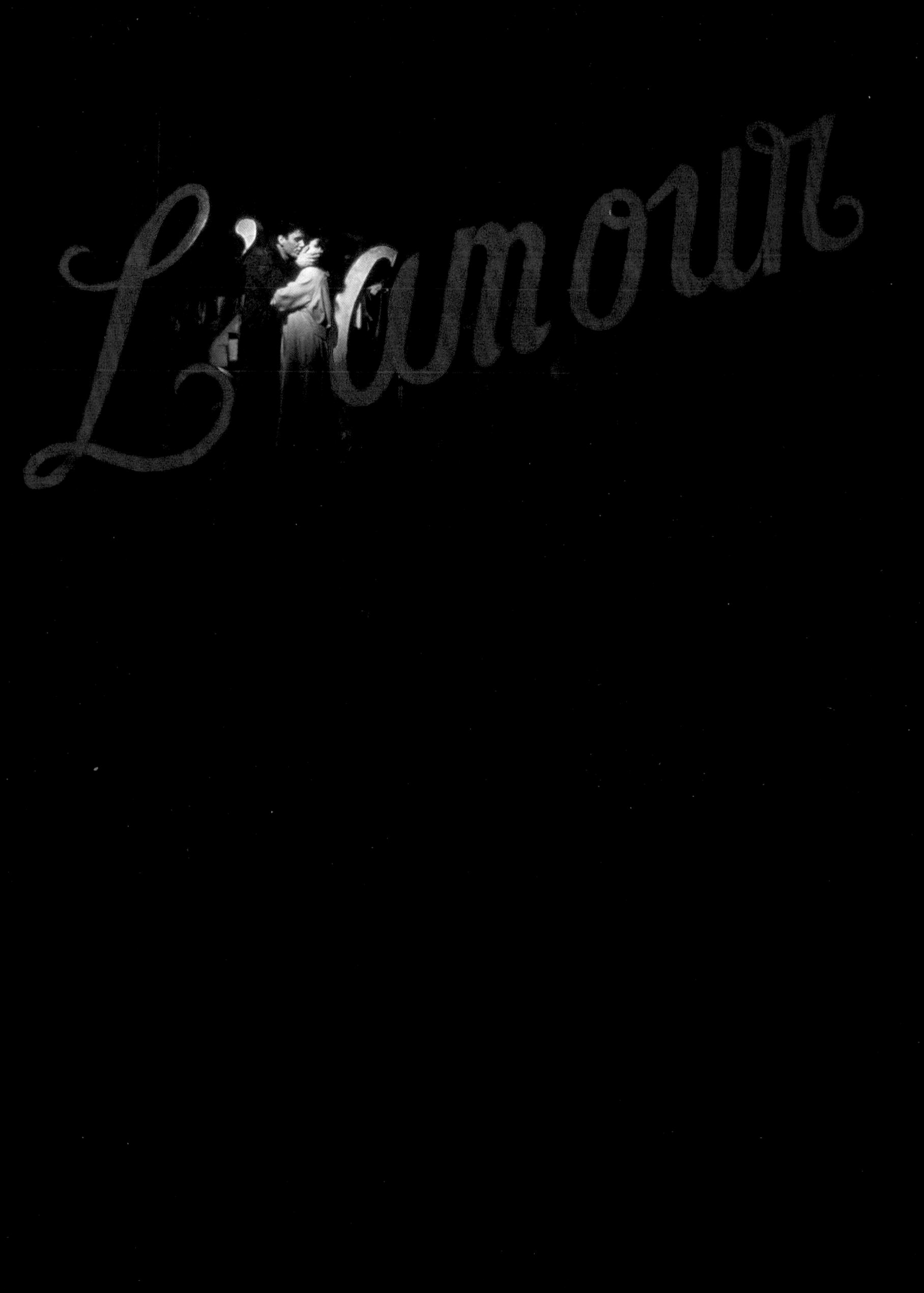
L'amour

FOREWORD

Louise Herron CEO

I always love hearing performers tell their audience how excited they are
to be on stage at the Sydney Opera House. I've heard so many artists who
perform routinely in the world's greatest venues – Leonard Cohen, Sharon
Van Etten, Nils Frahm, James Blake, Lizzo, Prince, Zubin Mehta, Joshua Bell,
David Hallberg, Brian Cox, even Bluey, to name just a few – speak of being
deeply moved by this place. The audience usually applauds because they
feel the same way. Even today, after more than a decade as the CEO of
this remarkable building, I am still inspired by its form, its star power and
its potential.

     As we approached the Opera House's 50th anniversary, we
wanted to capture that universal appeal. We invited accomplished artists
from Australia and around the world to reflect on their most memorable
and personal Opera House moments. From Nick Cave to Simone Young,
Richard Bonynge to Briggs, Clementine Ford to William Barton, these
stories focus on the unique qualities that make performing at the Opera
House such a transcendent experience.

     What the artists make clear is that there's always been something
magical about the Opera House, inside and out. The spirit soars in its
presence. Our recently completed Decade of Renewal was about setting
the stage for future generations of artists, audiences and visitors. Through
this book, we are not only celebrating half a century of unforgettable
moments but also inviting everyone to be part of the next fifty years.

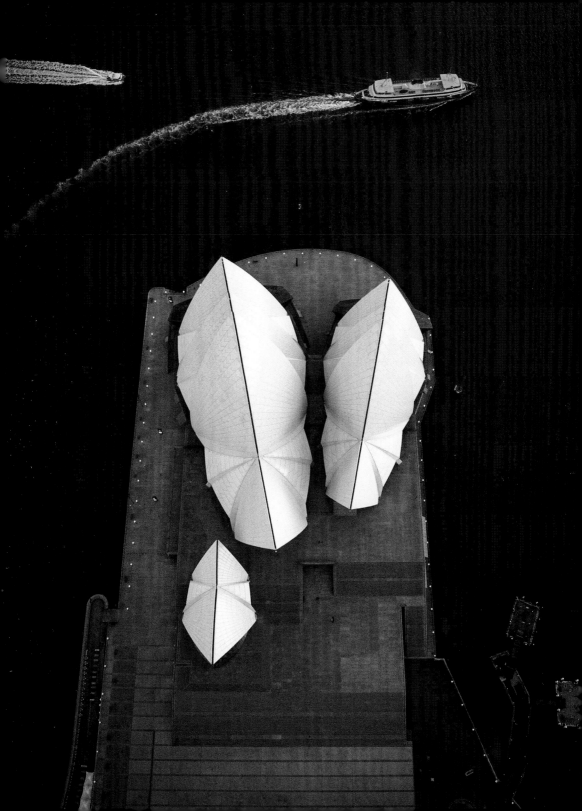

INTRODUCTION

Ashleigh Wilson Editor

It was a historic moment, and a long time coming. Queen Elizabeth stood on the podium, gripping her notes against the afternoon north-westerlies, and she spoke about culture, community and a building that reached to the sky. If she had looked into the faces of the dignitaries gathered for this grand occasion, the sense of relief would have been hard to miss. They had made it. Finally, the job was done. After years of delays and politics and creative tensions, the building was finished.

But the opening of the Sydney Opera House in October 1973 was only ever the start of this story. As the royal party left Bennelong Point that day, trailed by cameras and politicians and royal enthusiasts, a new era of cultural activity was stirring into life behind them. Here, at last, was the reason for all those years of work: a platform for imagination, connection and stories.

The Queen touched on this idea herself. The pyramids, she said, were universally admired despite the difficulties that had attended their construction. 'I believe this will be so for the Sydney Opera House,' she said. 'The Opera House will have something the pyramids never had – it will have life.'

As a building, Jørn Utzon's creation needs no introduction. Harry Seidler called it 'pure poetry'. Its inclusion on the UNESCO World Heritage list in 2007 did indeed put it alongside the pyramids, along with landmarks like the Great Wall of China, the Statue of Liberty and the Tower of London.

The architectural achievement is clear to all who gaze in wonder upon those sails. But when the curtain went up that day in 1973, its essential function came into view. Storytelling has always been the quality that separates the Opera House from other exalted monuments around the world. And it's through storytelling that the Opera House renews itself each day.

To mark the first half-century of the Opera House, we are bringing together fifty memories from fifty artists across fifty years, each one carrying with them a special, intangible connection to the building and its history. In their own way, these are transformative moments. They endure with a special kind of potency – raw, revelatory and powerfully alive. These are also stories that reveal as much about the Opera House as they do about the city itself.

From opera to hip-hop, contemporary dance to outdoor extravaganzas, we see artists and audiences engaging with memories both elusive and exhilarating. Every now and then, performer and audience come together as one to 'tug at the hem of the infinite to collude with the divine', to borrow the words of Nick Cave – and anyone lucky enough to have been there in the moment finds themselves truly blessed, touched by grace, some part of them changed forever.

This is, after all, the tragic beauty of live performance, this tension between impermanence and transcendence. These glimpses of eternity never to be repeated, never to be forgotten.

Bob Dylan, himself well-acquainted with the Concert Hall stage, calls it the 'shimmering persistence of memory'. In *The Philosophy of Modern Song*, he writes about the recurring familiarity that reverberates through the Rodgers and Hart classic 'Where or When' – and his observation could equally apply to any of today's artistic forms: '[It is] a thing with which to make memories and the memory itself.'

Dylan makes an appearance in these pages, but not in the way you might expect. Other relationships emerge across genres and generations: Jimmy Barnes transported by Billy Connolly to the streets of Glasgow; Paul Kelly electrified by Mozart; Ngaiire invoking Crowded House on the side of the Forecourt stage; Clementine Ford moved by the power of community; Simone Young watching Leonard Bernstein animate Tchaikovsky's Sixth Symphony.

Each artist was encouraged to identify a single moment that resonated with them through the years. The brief was deliberately broad.

Their memory could be drawn from the stage, while watching from the audience, even walking past the building.

For many of those who appear in this book, the choice was obvious. These were life-changing moments, after all. Sometimes, though, a single memory wasn't enough. Barrie Kosky, for instance, offers up the 'three postcards' that make up his personal collage. Jennie Begg – journalist, singer, Opera House enthusiast and indefatigable audience member over many years – witnessed half a century of activity up close, and her connection filters through her family as well. This has always been a house for the people, she writes, not just an elite few. It also continues a long tradition of community and storytelling on Tubowgule, a Gadigal meeting place for thousands of years. Peter Gilmore, one of Australia's most celebrated culinary artists, feels a kind of awe while working in the presence of this history.

Actors, singers, writers, directors, designers, composers, rappers, choreographers, conductors, visual artists, producers, dancers: everyone, it seems, has an Opera House story all of their own. And these are stories that exist beyond words, too. Hence the contribution of Tim Sharp, a widely admired artist with autism who created the superhero Laser Beak Man, himself a regular visitor to this building.

Certain themes emerge. Some memories take us back to the Olympic Arts Festival in 2000, recalling the joyful spirit that spread throughout the city. Another recurring figure is La Stupenda herself, Dame Joan Sutherland, on stage and off. More than three decades have passed since her final performance in a full-length opera, and Richard Bonynge can still feel the caress of the streamers that fell from the Opera Theatre ceiling as *Les Huguenots* brought this story to an end. Twelve years later, that theatre was renamed in her honour.

The most common sentiment is the majesty of the building itself, and how that majesty contributes to the creativity around it. Bill Henson hears a sacred hymn when he looks upon the Opera House, and he's visited enough cities around the world to know this is rare in the modern age. Artists sense it when they come to perform. Audiences sense it, too. If the Opera House is a cathedral, a temple for culture, then elevated experiences are the result. Of course, the stories that follow make up only a small part of this sustained hymn of transcendence. Each of us feels that pulse in our own way.

Following spread_ Club Kooky on the Northern Broadwalk
as part of Vivid LIVE 2022. Photo: Daniel Boud.

3

PAUL KELLY

It's a heart-stopping building. I lived in Sydney between 1984 and 1990 and toured a lot in that time, often travelling north. Coming back into the city after a series of shows, having driven through the interminable northern suburbs, suddenly we would swing down onto the freeway from Crows Nest, and there out to the left on Bennelong Point would be those dreaming sails that would, in Seamus Heaney's words, 'catch the heart off guard and blow it open'.

I'd been close to the building, if 'building' is what you could call it. I'd walked around it, wondering at the irregular size of the tiles. I'd caught the ferry from Circular Quay to Manly and seen it singing in the light on the way home, but I hadn't been inside it and had never seen a show there. Money was too tight to mention.

In 1987, I received my first royalty cheque. It was more money than I'd ever been paid at one time. I did two things. I bought myself a gold electric guitar from a music shop on Parramatta Road and then three tickets for me, my sister and a housemate to Mozart's opera *Don Giovanni* at the Sydney Opera House.

Both my grandparents on my mother's side sang Italian opera. Ercole and Nance Filippini. They didn't just sing it; they produced it. During the 1920s and 30s, they toured opera around Australia on a shoestring budget, long before the days of government subsidies. They travelled by train up the Queensland coast, through towns where many migrant Italians worked, cutting cane in fierce heat to put sugar in everybody's tea and cake. All the way to Cairns and down and then west to Longreach. No orchestra. Just one piano player, two violins, a handful of singers and a volunteer chorus. Then later on to South Australia and Western Australia.

Above_ John Wegner in Opera Australia's *Don Giovanni*, 1987.
Photo: Branco Gaica. Courtesy of Opera Australia.
Following spread_ Paul Kelly performs on the Opera House
Forecourt in 2017. Photo: Prudence Upton.

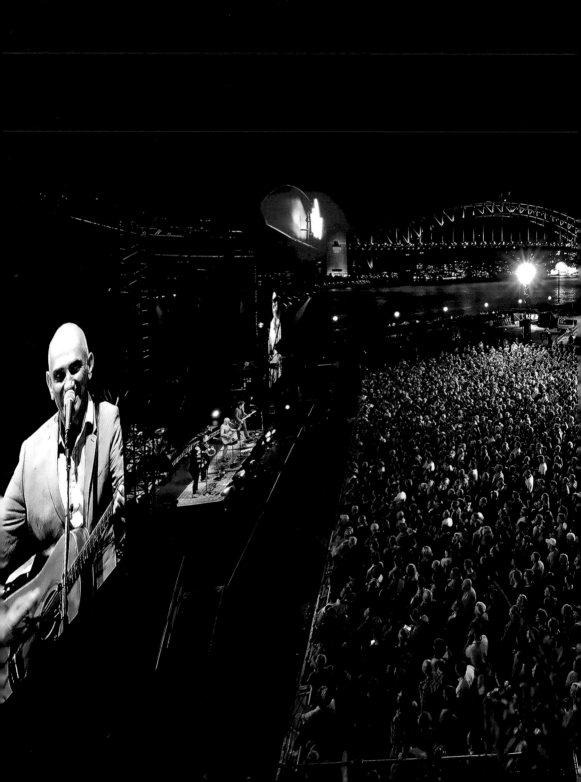

They gave singing lessons and mounted shows, incorporating their students into the chorus, expanded the orchestra, and called themselves the Italo-Australian Grand Opera Company. Their dreams were grand but their income stream less so. Still, they scraped by. Money too tight to mention. Tighter, even when Ercole died from ulcer complications in 1934.

So, I'd grown up with opera in the air. My grandparents' story was family lore. Mum and Dad had records of classical music and there were concerts on the ABC in the evenings and weekends. Though I was a sports-mad child – cricket, football, tennis, swimming – somehow that music poured into me like milk.

I was proud and excited to be shouting my big sister, Anne, and my friend Irene to the opera. Anne had been but Irene never had, nor I.

We took our seats. The lights dimmed. The overture began with those two big, long chords of doom. Instantly, I was electrified and, if memory serves me well, which it doesn't always, for the next three hours I didn't leave the edge of my seat.

Leporello is the first character we see on stage and the first voice we hear. Don Giovanni's conflicted and put-upon servant, his enabler and moral critic. It's a role my grandfather, Ercole, a baritone, would have played. Leporello getting into scrapes through trying to help his master out of scrapes is a constant theme of the story.

There is a murder right at the start as Don Giovanni attempts to extricate himself from an assignation with Donna Anna. In doing so, he kills her father, the Commendatore, and the wheels of revenge are set in motion.

I won't try to describe the plot. In time-honoured opera tradition, it is convoluted and ridiculous. Throughout, Don tries to seduce every woman he meets, highborn and low, in streets, mansions and gardens. None of them are too wise. He has no redeeming qualities. He lies, connives, bullies, acts violently and has no compunction setting up his faithful servant to be killed in order to spare his own life. (Thankfully that doesn't happen.)

But he can sing. That night, just as the Don's thrilling, seductive tenor melted all resistance, so too did Mozart's music flood my whole being. I'd heard the music before – much of it had a deep familiarity – but to see the characters in the flesh, their voices intertwining, was a whole different experience.

Afire in the dark, I was reminded of the first time I heard early New Orleans jazz. Another sister's boyfriend had brought some Louis

Armstrong and The Hot Five records to the house when I was thirteen years old and learning the trumpet. Hearing that music blew the roof off my head. Every instrument seemed to be doing its own thing unrelated to the others, but somehow all the chaos made beautiful sense.

So, too, that night. For the first time I really saw and heard the genius of opera, and in particular, Mozart. Tawdry to glory. One character would start singing, then another. And another. And so on. Sometimes they sang to each other, sometimes with each other, sometimes at cross purposes, sometimes as an aside to the audience. The tendril of a simple, gorgeous melody would build into an intricate forest of sound with four characters singing different melodies, different rhythms and different words with different intentions. The tenors, the sopranos, the baritone, the bass. Joining up, flying off, joining back. Again, the roof blew off my head.

Then, when the ghost of the Commendatore appeared right near the end singing 'Don Giovanni!' in a voice of deep doom, I swear my body left the chair. 'Repent!' commanded the Commendatore. But Don, like Shakespeare's Richard III, who also delighted in his wickedness, cunning and power, was not for turning. Defiantly he consigned himself to the flames.

I didn't want to leave the theatre as the lights came up. I wanted to stay in the spell with the Don in the fiery furnace. 'Bravo to him!' I exclaimed to Anne and Irene as we slowly left our seats. 'He stayed true to his terrible self. You have to admire that.'

Anne still teases me to this day. 'I'll never forget the expression on your face at the end of *Don Giovanni*,' she says. 'Your eyes were blazing! You loved him, didn't you?' True, I did. True, I do.

That's what opera can do to you.

___ Paul Kelly is one of Australia's great singer-songwriters. His music has provided the soundtrack to multiple generations, from his early years on the Melbourne band scene and his breakthrough 80s hits to his evergreen 90s classics and generous collaborations with the new guard of Australian music.

SIMONE YOUNG

Unless you grow up in a musician's household, your first experiences in a major hall, with a major orchestra, stay with you for a lifetime. It's such an overwhelming, physical thing.

There was a charming naivety to what happened here. In August 1974, the ABC was about to film Leonard Bernstein's New York Philharmonic on stage at the Sydney Opera House, and they were giving away tickets. A friend of my mother's had a spare ticket, and it must have been school holidays, so I was roped in as her spare. We sat up in the gods – a typical conductor, I now see everything from my point of view, so if you're looking from the podium, we were in the far upper left-hand corner. I had no idea who Bernstein was and only a vague idea what the New York Philharmonic represented. My family had bought a record player just a few months earlier, and I'd started collecting records at church fetes, but this was the first time I had attended a symphony concert.

When Bernstein came out with the New York Philharmonic, they played Tchaikovsky's Sixth Symphony, the *Pathétique*, and I was completely blown away. Almost always, when you perform the third movement, there's a lot of applause at the end, because it's incredibly rousing. It's powerful, uplifting, energetic. Usually as a conductor, you launch into the drama and the tragedy of the fourth movement, cutting into the applause, and that's what Lenny did. The last movement is relatively short, only about nine minutes, but we felt devastated by the time we reached the end. It's exhausting, a huge emotional journey, and even for a newcomer like me, to sit in this incredible hall in this amazing building, watching one of the world's great orchestras, I knew this was a big deal.

They took their bows, and Bernstein went off stage. Then a chap from the ABC came on and told us, incredibly apologetically, that they were going to have to play the third and fourth movements again because a baby had cried during the performance. You can only imagine the cheer that went up in the hall. It was incredibly exciting.

At that point in my life, I was a typical, convent-taught pianist; the most dramatic thing I had played was a Beethoven piano sonata. After that concert, the first thing I did was go out and buy a recording: it had one of those ghastly 70s covers but it happened to be Yevgeny Mravinsky conducting Tchaikovsky Six. That and Bernstein's are still my favourite Tchaikovsky Six recordings. It's my favourite symphony, too. It was the first I conducted, in rehearsal in Cologne, and I've conducted it many times since. I've done it twice at the Opera House, the first time in 2011, for the inaugural concert of the Australian World Orchestra, and the second in 2022, as part of my first season with the Sydney Symphony Orchestra. I love every note of it.

The New York Philharmonic Orchestra, conducted by Leonard Bernstein, in the Concert Hall, 1974. Photo courtesy of The New York Philharmonic Shelby White & Leon Levy Digital Archives.

I was born in 1961, so I spent my childhood watching the Opera House being built. We lived in Balgowlah and my dad worked in the city, and we passed Bennelong Point on the Manly Ferry many, many times. I first performed there in 1975 as a schoolkid in a City of Sydney Eisteddfod, and my school had its 100th anniversary show in the Concert Hall. My first orchestral concert was there, then I ran the opera company, and now I'm running the symphony, so it's really been my whole life.

Unless you grow up in a musician's household, your first experiences in a major hall, with a major orchestra, stay with you for a lifetime. It's such an overwhelming, physical thing. It's not just emotional: it hits you in the core of your body. If the first chord of the fourth movement – that searing, painful chord that cuts in on all the military excess and triumph of the third – doesn't feel like a punch to your stomach, then you've got the emotional range of a teaspoon, as Hermione puts it in Harry Potter. That's why it was doubly poetic and significant for me to come home to the orchestra, and also to come home to the Concert Hall, with its extraordinary new transformation. It's like a whole new hall. It's like having that experience all over again.

— Simone Young AM is one of the most prestigious conductors of her generation. Before taking over as chief conductor of the Sydney Symphony in 2022, she had held many leadership roles around the world, including general manager and music director of the Hamburg State Opera; music director of the Philharmonic State Orchestra Hamburg; music director of Opera Australia; chief conductor of the Bergen Philharmonic Orchestra; and principal guest conductor of the Orchestre de Chambre de Lausanne.

LI CUNXIN

Mary McKendry and I had met in London and married in Houston, where we were principal dancers with the Houston Ballet. By 1989, we had just welcomed our first child, Sophie, when an invitation came from Sydney. The Australian Ballet, then under Maina Gielgud's directorship, was about to put on an international gala at the Sydney Opera House starring Australian dancers who had been successful around the world. One of the dancers they wanted to perform was Mary, who had been born in Rockhampton before moving to Europe as a teenager to study at The Royal Ballet School.

The Australian Ballet asked her to dance with Ross Stretton, who at the time was a principal dancer with the American Ballet Theatre. Mary asked Noel Pelly, the company's general manager, if he would consider her husband instead. 'He's a wonderful dancer,' she said, 'and he's also half-Australian because he's married to me.' But no. They wanted Australians, so that was that. But a week before rehearsals, Stretton injured himself, and an opportunity emerged. Out of desperation or convenience, the company asked whether I was still available and willing to join Mary in Sydney as her partner.

Mary McKendry and Li Cunxin dancing the *Esmeralda* pas de deux for The Australian
Ballet, Concert Hall, 1990. Photo: Branco Gaica. Courtesy of The Australian Ballet.

Obviously I had been aware of the stature and beauty and significance of the Opera House – I'd seen photos, and Mary had made me familiar with it – but to actually look at the structure and to walk up the steps ahead of that performance gave me chills. The majesty, the beauty: I remember that wonderful first day very clearly, and I can still picture the sunshine, the tiles glistening in the sun, the water. What a scene. And then we danced, and it just felt so special.

The gala was held on 22 November 1990, and we danced the famous *Esmeralda* pas de deux. The audience was incredibly responsive. When you perform in a space with rich traditions and stories attached to it like the Opera House, it makes the occasion even more meaningful.

My association with the building grew from there. Five years later, I joined The Australian Ballet as a principal artist, and one of my favourite parts of the job was to perform at the Opera House each year. And when the time came for my very last dance, Basilio in Rudolf Nureyev's *Don Quixote*, in April 1999, that was where it had to be. At the end of the night, when I looked into the mirror, when I took off my make-up for the last time, I was very emotional. The surroundings and the symmetry only added to the sense of occasion: the first time I had danced in Australia, and the end of my career, had both taken place at the Opera House.

There's another story I can't resist sharing. In 2016, I was asked to interview Jackie Chan, the actor and martial arts star, for a Talks & Ideas event at the Opera House. At that point, I was artistic director of Queensland Ballet, but I was also a huge Jackie Chan fan, and we were scheduled to appear together in conversation on the Concert Hall stage. Before the talk, we met in the dressing room, and I told him how much I loved his films and he congratulated me for *Mao's Last Dancer*, the book that had been turned into a movie. Then he asked where my people were. He had a whole entourage around him and I had come alone. I didn't have an entourage like him, of course. It was just me.

The surroundings and the symmetry only added to the sense of occasion: the first time I had danced in Australia, and the end of my career, had both taken place at the Opera House.

__Li Cunxin AO took over as artistic director of Queensland Ballet in 2013 and announced his retirement in 2023. After he was selected by Madame Mao's cultural advisors to attend the Beijing Dance Academy at the age of eleven, he went on to become a principal dancer at Houston Ballet before moving to Melbourne in 1995 to join The Australian Ballet as a principal artist. In 2003 he published his international best-selling autobiography *Mao's Last Dancer*, which was adapted as a feature film six years later.

KATE FITZPATRICK

As I lay there, my shin
bleeding, the audience
was told there would
be a delay.

In 1966, newly arrived from Adelaide, I joined the Bring Back Utzon marches in Sydney. We wanted Jørn Utzon, the Danish architect who had just left the project following a dispute with the government, to sort the scaffolding and chaos on the foreshore.

The following year, John Clark, the NIDA tutor who was soon to become its director, took second-year students on a tour of the building. It was my birthday. There were still cranes but most of the scaffolding was down. The shells were being tiled. It was fascinating: a butterfly emerging from its spiky chrysalis.

There were two sorts of cream tile, glazed and dull. Necessary so the shells would gleam but not blind. I was given one as a present. Still have it. Inside was raw and beautiful. Just the concrete structure, no lining or fittings. I felt safe. Protected, like Jonah. Waiting for those incredible ribs to breathe with me.

The Drama Theatre was a shock. It seemed to house an empty swimming pool. No water. Just a deep hole. No one knew why. We were assured it would be sorted before the opening. At the end was a giant letterbox opening, one day to become the proscenium and stage.

Five years later, Jim Sharman's *The Threepenny Opera* company moved in to open the Drama Theatre. I had never been so excited about going to work. The House, as it was already called, looked magnificent. A half-opened fan of giant pearl shells decorating an ancient oyster midden. We knew the history, and were happy that this building, surrounded by water, like a ship, was finally a place everyone could enjoy.

Everything was new and shiny and smelled wonderful. Ours were the first faces to look into those dressing room mirrors and hope for the best. It became our home away from home, and we quickly made ourselves comfortable.

On the first day, someone broke a toilet seat. Apparently all the fittings were unique, so we pretended it hadn't happened. Another of our company took the first shower. Only when soapy water seeped under the door, soaking the carpet, did we realise there was no protection between bathroom tiles and carpet. In the ensuing months our room stank and frilly mushrooms grew up the wall. It was also rumoured that another company member was the first to fall in, and subsequently make, love in the House. In an Opera Theatre box, the story went, with one of the cast from *War and Peace*.

The atmosphere was electric. We had never mixed en masse with opera singers, ballet dancers and musicians before. We watched each other rehearse and perform. We shared terrible canteen meals, admiration, gossip and history.

The Queen came. I didn't see the fireworks because I was on stage as Pirate Jenny. From there, I could see the Black Freighter coming up the dark green night harbour outside. I believed the audience could, too. This was more than a building. It was alive. We had given it a heart, lungs and a soul.

But my most memorable performance was in February 1979, the night I fell down a trapdoor. I was Marguerite Gautier in *The Lady of the Camellias*. Fabulous costumes. Full houses. Audience members sobbing at the curtain call.

The set piece was a sumptuous circular bed. As the audience took their seats, the bed was on their side of the fire curtain. A six-foot rectangular trench had been cut into the stage so it could be moved back as the curtain rose, covering the trap. That night I was early. The stage working lights were still on. I could see Annie Byron, playing my maid, in the opposite prompt wings and decided to run across the stage. To make her laugh, I turned towards the unseeing audience and stuck my tongue out, but in the process fell down the trap. As I lay there, my shin bleeding, the audience was told there would be a delay. I was flipped over. In order to keep blood off my voluminous silk and lace skirts, garments were lifted over my head. As a secret joke, the director, Rex Cramphorn, had suggested I shouldn't wear knickers. Courtesans didn't, for obvious reasons. No one would ever know.

There came a quiet but audible gasp from the seventeen actors and stagehands staring down at me. I was wearing cream satin shoes, white silk stockings held up by ribboned garters, and had quite a lot of blood seeping from my left shin. But above my knees to where my corset ended: just my birthday suit. I lay there like Magritte's mother after she'd been dragged from the river Sambre, her nightgown over her head. The nurse worked on my leg, bandaged my shin and gave me an injection for the pain (but nothing for the mortification). Plus, a new stocking and different shoes. I was hauled to my feet. My skirt was rearranged. Still knicker-less, I assumed my wing position and watched as the lights dimmed, the music started, the audience shushed, the curtain went up and the bed slid back to cover the trap.

__ Kate Fitzpatrick is a stage and film actor and writer. A NIDA graduate, she has appeared in twenty films and 110 plays including *The Threepenny Opera*, *The Rocky Horror Show*, *The Lady of the Camellias*, *Cabaret*, Patrick White's *The Season at Sarsaparilla* and *Big Toys*, which White wrote for her. Her first book was the 2010 memoir *Name Dropping*. She was awarded the Queen Elizabeth II Silver Jubilee Medal in 1977 for services to the theatre.

BRIGGS

It was a good barometer
for the next generation, for
the young artists to think
this is achievable, that
this can be our house.

Above and on the following spread_ Briggs' Bad Apples
House Party, Vivid LIVE, 2019. Photos: Daniel Boud.

This was our opportunity to make something to remember. We knew what we had to do. We couldn't waste this stage. We had to do something that made sense. Something dope.

Briggs' Bad Apples House Party, part of Vivid LIVE in 2019, was our moment to cement the label, the artistry, as the real thing. There had been very little rap music at the Opera House to that point. I'd seen Ice Cube, I'd seen Wu-Tang Clan – in fact, I interviewed RZA on the steps in the northern foyer – so I'd always been floating around. But it wasn't really a space for rap music.

We knew about the prestige of the place. We knew it was going to amplify these young Indigenous artists from around the country. We were going to make that stage ours. The Opera House, one of the most prestigious buildings in the world, not just in the country – this was our house. But it wasn't until the day itself, when we were wandering around the rabbit warren out the back of the Joan Sutherland Theatre – where I ran into Robert Smith from The Cure; they were playing next door in the Concert Hall – that it hit us.

Everything is elevated when you're at the Opera House, but you need to adapt to the situation. The crowd isn't as free to move around like they are in other venues. If they step out to the bar, they miss it. We made it the biggest house party we could think of. There were a lot of different artists on the bill; we wanted it to be collaborative.

It was a good barometer for the next generation, for the young artists to think this is achievable, that this can be our house. That's what I've tried to do from the start of my career. We have this stage, this captive audience, and we're going to reach people we've never reached before, so we better have something to say. You can't waste these opportunities. We seldom get a second shot, so let's do this thing for real. Let's make it worthwhile and make them ask for it again.

This was a real achievement for the record label. And it foreshadowed First & Forever, our new festival that kicked off in Hanging Rock to celebrate First Nations culture and music. That eclectic mix of artists is what we're always trying to capture with a Bad Apples House Party: the talent of Indigenous artists, the wide spectrum on which we exist. It's not just one homogenous sound and point of view.

So the significance of the occasion was never lost on me. It was an opportunity to make this our own, to make it something to remember. But on the day, you have to put all that in the back of your head; otherwise you're going to be dwarfed by the house itself. I'd been doing this for so many years, and a stage is a stage. I've got a job to do, and I can't get lost in the hype. But when you've got younger artists around who haven't done all that, and they're all super excited, full of wonder and buzzing, it's a great vibe. It was like Christmas.

Backstage, there was a lot of joy, and I was feeding off that energy. They were stoked. I've been around the world, but sometimes you forget. A lot of these kids who live in Sydney may have only been to the Opera House on a school excursion or seen it when going past on a train. Even though it's your city, it can still be kind of unattainable. And then, suddenly, we cracked the door open. It was like we'd snuck in. The Cure was next door, doing their thing, and we were over here, doing our thing. It was like: Mum and Dad are out, let's go.

__ A musician, writer, actor and entrepreneur, Yorta Yorta hip-hop artist Briggs, or Adam Briggs, won plaudits as a solo rapper before co-founding the award-winning duo AB Original in 2016. He founded the Indigenous hip-hop record label Bad Apples Music and is the chair of the Adam Briggs Foundation, nurturing First Nations excellence in the creative industries.

CLEMENTINE FORD

All those who walk the boards here have been filled by the magic of those who came before and left some of their own behind for those who come after. The work lives on, long after the artists have stepped back into the shadows.

Clementine Ford at the All About Women festival,
Utzon Room, 2023. Photo: Cassandra Hannagan.

My first time on stage at the Sydney Opera House more or less coincided with the period of my professional life in which I was invited to appear on ABC TV's *Q&A* program. I was newly into writing a regular column for a paper that used to be good and is now bad, and was becoming associated with what my grandmother might have politely referred to as 'strident views'. In response to the *Q&A* appearance, a conservative tabloid writer described me as 'just some feminist with bared tattoos', the suggestion being that women like me had no place in Serious Discussions.

But in response to the columns, the Opera House invited me to speak at its inaugural All About Women festival in April 2013. Truthfully, I can't remember the specifics of what we discussed on that first full day of talks and panels. What I do remember was the excitement that filled not just the various theatrettes and main stages of this gloriously incomprehensible building, but also snapped, crackled and popped through the foyers, down the stairs and out the doors. The place was alive with women, many of whom were attending their first proudly feminist event. I saw women talking animatedly with their friends; teenage daughters with guards tentatively down, paying rare attention to their mothers who were trying not to spook them into closing the shutters once again; chubby-cheeked babies being whispered a promise of change from elderly women living to fight another day; even the occasional man, listening in the audience.

It was the feeling, finally, that feminism was back.

As a passionate and occasionally hot-headed (me? unlikely!) student feminist wallowing in the cultural wasteland of the aughts, I had grown used to hearing the opposite: feminism was over. Didn't we know we'd won? Women could do anything now, as long as it never, ever made men feel even slightly uncomfortable!

Equality, baby. Who knew it was that easy?

But the teen years of the 21st century brought a new hunger for voices; our voices. Julia Gillard's prime ministership was under constant attack from misogynists, all of whom would act further aghast at even the suggestion they had a shred of sexism in them. In a series of devastating and high-profile cases, men's violence against women came to the fore, making it harder to ignore the fact that nowhere – homes, parks or busy city streets – was safe for us. Young women, those divine creatures of rage and change, were ready for the fight once again. And the Opera

House welcomed them all, year after year, providing a space for courage to release its call.

Having now reached my middle years, I am wise enough to know that each generation fighting for feminist liberation will bring with them their own passions, persuasions and political goals. How lucky we all are to have the opportunity to hear what they have to say, and to join in conversation with them.

The Opera House sails into the harbour of each of its lovers' hearts in different ways. But for me, this place will always be one in which women have been able to find joy and support in each other's company, and to be energetically charged for what comes next. It has been my extraordinary privilege to appear at almost every All About Women festival, speaking with luminaries such as Roxane Gay, Tishani Doshi, Germaine Greer, Chanel Miller, Anne Summers and many more. These women have fundamentally changed the feminist landscape, and with it, the possibilities the world holds for each of us. I think that, in my own way, I have done the same.

I believe places hold onto the energy of all they have seen and given life to. All those who walk the boards here have been filled by the magic of those who came before and left some of their own behind for those who come after. The work lives on, long after the artists have stepped back into the shadows.

In this hallowed space, I have been and become many things. A passionate speaker. A comedian. A friend. An interrogator. A writer. A mother. A singer. A lover. A fighter. And yes, just another feminist with bared tattoos – one of many, in fact. Women just like me, who found themselves in a place just like this.

__ Clementine Ford is an award-winning writer and performer living in Naarm/Melbourne. The best-selling author of three non-fiction titles, her latest polemic, *I Don't: The Case Against Marriage*, is published through Allen & Unwin. She is one half of the performance team behind *Love Sermon*, which debuted at the Sydney Opera House before going on to enjoy a sold-out national tour. She is currently developing a narrative fiction series for television.

IVA DAVIES

To be among the first to
perform in the new Opera
House was an unimaginable
inspiration.

Iva Davies in the Sydney Dance Company's *Berlin*,
choreographed by Graeme Murphy, Drama Theatre, 1995.
Photo: Branco Gaica. Courtesy of Sydney Dance Company.

When I wrote the opening lines to 'Great Southern Land' in 1982 – 'city on a rainy day down in the harbour' I was thinking of a number of Australia's harbour cities. But by far the central picture I had in mind went back to me at about fourteen or fifteen as I stepped off a train that had carried me for forty-five minutes from Sydney suburbia to the platform at Circular Quay. Looking out, I scanned the harbour as the rain drizzled down. The scene was dominated by an extraordinary building, as yet incomplete, and teams of bustling workers at the building site amid piles of building steel, conveyor belts of concrete trucks, and all this under a grey sky, as a future icon was being finished.

I'd auditioned for, and won, a scholarship to the NSW Conservatorium of Music as an oboist. And this is how I found myself on that platform. A short trudge up the hill to Macquarie Street took me to my first lesson at the Conservatorium, and every Thursday afternoon after school from then.

Every week I looked out across that scene and watched the progress of the work on the Opera House. From a series of raw but imposing concrete shells I saw the addition of glistening pearl white tiles and vast panels of gleaming glass, while inside the details of wood panelling, acres of carpet and rows of plush chairs were being installed.

By the time I'd finished school and successfully auditioned at the Con as a full-time tertiary oboe student, the Opera House was nearly complete. I was made a member of the Conservatorium Senior Orchestra, and we rehearsed every week. In early 1973, the orchestra was advised we would be teaming up with the Conservatorium Opera School to perform two one-act Australian operas. The extraordinary part was this: we would be performing in the new Sydney Opera House.

On 25 and 28 July 1973, we performed *The Fall of the House of Usher* by Larry Sitsky and *Dalgerie* by James Penberthy. This was three months before the 'official' opening by the Queen and The Australian Opera's performance of Prokofiev's *War and Peace*, which is always claimed as the first opera performed in the Opera House.

Although it was not a celebrated occasion, I believe it was important for two reasons. Firstly, these two works were Australian operas, composed by Australian composers and librettists. Secondly, perhaps even more importantly, they were performed by young Australians. Some were semi-professional students like myself, but all had aspirations and were striving for a future in music. To be among the first to perform in the new Opera House was an unimaginable inspiration. I was just eighteen at the time.

I went on to play there many times, as an oboist with the Sydney Symphony Orchestra and also accompanying the Philharmonia Choirs in the Concert Hall, with various ensembles in the smaller Music Room and later on in the Opera Theatre once again.

By a strange twist, my classical career was unexpectedly cut short around 1975, and the odd path I took led me to start a punk rock'n'roll band in 1977 called Flowers. That band was renamed ICEHOUSE and went on to achieve international success. During my ICEHOUSE career, I composed two ballet scores for the Sydney Dance Company. Along with my band, I performed those scores live, and both ballets opened at the Opera Theatre (*Boxes* in 1985, *Berlin* in 1995).

Then in 1999, I was commissioned by the City of Sydney to expand 'Great Southern Land' into a 25-minute piece to be performed on the Northern Forecourt in the minutes leading Australia into the new millennium. The expanded piece, 'The Ghost of Time', took the form of a double concerto featuring Richard Tognetti on electric violin, myself on electric guitar, the Sydney Symphony Orchestra and Taikoz – an ensemble of Australian percussionists specialising in Japanese taiko drums.

It was an unbelievably exciting place to be. The piece finished, the television presenter started counting – 'Ten, nine, eight …' – and the fireworks went off above my head. The performance for the more than a million people assembled around the harbour that night was also broadcast live to an estimated four billion people worldwide.

Finally, at the end of 2022, the final ICEHOUSE performance celebrating the fortieth anniversary of 'Great Southern Land' was scheduled to take place on the Forecourt. Heartbreakingly, I caught COVID-19 just before the show and had to cancel, though we were quickly making plans to return. Hopefully that day won't be a 'rainy day down in the harbour'.

— Iva Davies AM is an Australian singer, songwriter and producer, best known as the lead singer and founder of ICEHOUSE, as well as a composer of successful ballet scores and multi-award-winning soundtracks.

WAYNE BLAIR

I wanted to give it a red-hot go. And then, after all my cajoling about drama school and living in Sydney, it took the lady from *Mother and Son* for my parents to finally relax.

Margaret Harvey, Wayne Blair and Ursula Yovich in *The Sunshine Club*, at the Drama Theatre in 2000, produced by Sydney Theatre Company, in association with Sydney Festival and Sydney Opera House Trust, and by arrangement with Queensland Theatre Company. Photo: Tracey Schramm. Courtesy of Sydney Theatre Company.

I was twenty-eight, and had only just graduated from drama school, when I landed my first mainstage production. The show was called *The Sunshine Club*, a new musical. Music by John Rodgers, words by Wesley Enoch. The Sydney Theatre Company and Queensland Theatre Company were bringing it to the Opera House as part of the Sydney Festival in January 2000. The show had already had its Queensland debut and I felt fortunate just to be a part of this production. The story seemed like a gift to the world and to perform in the Opera House was like playing State of Origin at Lang Park – for me anyway.

The story, set in 1960s Brisbane, was about the Sunshine Club, a place where Aboriginal people could feel at home, and Black and white people could gather freely, dance and just *be*. My character was Dave Daylight, and it was a great cast: Ursula Yovich, Peter Carroll, Elaine Crombie, Margaret Harvey, Simon Pryce, to name a few. It was like family.

My mum and dad travelled all the way down from Rockhampton for opening night. It was their first time at the Opera House and they probably had house seats. Even though their son was in the show, I'm pretty sure they didn't have any idea what was about to hit them.

At that point in my life, being an actor was still foreign to me, but it was even more foreign to my parents. They had wanted me to stay in Rockhampton, to work a normal job and be close to family and friends. To make it work in this industry, I had to make a deliberate decision to separate myself from my family.

On opening night, we received a standing ovation, and it was lovely. After the show, I had my shower, got my go-get-ems on and headed off to the afterparty. Before I caught up with friends, my first thought was to find Mum and Dad. Looking for them for a little while, suddenly I found them, and who should they be talking to? None other than Jacki Weaver and Ruth Cracknell, both of whom had come to the show that night. I joined in the conversation, and Jacki and Ruth were very pleasant with their feedback on the whole show.

I'll always remember what happened next. As they were leaving, Ruth turned to my parents and said: 'Bob, Julie, that boy of yours, I tell you what. After seeing him on that Opera House stage tonight, he might have a career in this acting caper, mark my words.'

'…that boy of yours, I tell you what. After seeing him on that Opera House stage tonight, he might have a career in this acting caper, mark my words.'

Being an actor is hard. You have to move away from home, there's no real support, and the work isn't at all consistent. I had to convince Mum and Dad that the industry was right for me. I didn't want to die wondering. I wanted to give it a red-hot go. And then, after all my cajoling about drama school and living in Sydney, it took the lady from *Mother and Son* for my parents to finally relax. After that, Dad said to me: 'I reckon you should pursue this "acting caper" more. Maybe you don't need to come back to Rocky for a few more years.'

— Wayne Blair is an award-winning actor, director and producer who works variously across film, television and theatre. His debut film as a director, *The Sapphires*, had its premiere at the Cannes Film Festival in 2012.

KITTY FLANAGAN

Unfortunately, there's not really anything funny about comedy gigs that go well. So, instead, let's go back to the very first time I played at the Sydney Opera House.

It was a last-minute thing. A slot came up at the Playhouse in August 2010 because my management had someone bigger and better playing in there at 9 pm, but the space was available at 7 pm. Would I like to do my own one-hour show? At the Opera House? Are you kidding? Of course, I would. I'm not an idiot. Or am I?

I had only recently returned to Australia after eight years of living and working in the UK. I wasn't on the telly and I didn't have much of a profile. What I'm saying is, I was not exactly a hot ticket item. There wasn't a lot of buzz on the street about Kitty Flanagan's first solo show at the Opera House. I, on the other hand, couldn't have been more excited. So much so, that I wanted to film the gig. I figured this might be my one and only chance to ever play the Opera House, so we should document it. We brought in cameras, we brought in chandeliers, I brought in my sister Penny to sing a big number to close the show and we had my ten-year-old nephew backstage as our roadie. It was a real moment.

Kitty Flanagan. Photo: Rebecca Bana.
Courtesy of A-List Entertainment.

I basically took to the stage wrapped in a double layer of compression bandages, unable to breathe properly, then babbled and wheezed at a room full of bemused tourists.

And it just kept getting better. Ticket sales had really picked up last minute. The room was full. I'd sold out the Opera House! What I didn't realise then was that playing such an iconic venue pretty much guarantees you an audience. Everyone who comes to Sydney wants to see the Opera House and a lot of those people also want to see something *at* the Opera House.

That night, I was that something. The Sydney Symphony Orchestra was sold out and the Joan Sutherland Theatre was at capacity. As a result, a few busloads of unsuspecting Japanese tourists ended up at my show. And to those people I say, *shazai itashimasu.* I am deeply sorry.

See, I talk pretty fast even when I'm not nervous. But when I'm nervous, dear god, good luck keeping up even if English is your first language. And I was nervous. Added to that, I'd had a last-minute panic about the camera 'adding ten pounds' and decided I should wear heavy-duty Spanx under what was already a very tight pair of black denim jeans. I basically took to the stage wrapped in a double layer of compression bandages, unable to breathe properly, then babbled and wheezed at a room full of bemused tourists. That's what I should have called the show: *Kitty Flanagan – Babble & Wheeze.* And then came the big finish. Because it was the Opera House, I had upped the ante and co-opted a choir to join me and my sister for the musical finale. A fabulous all-male choir, called Manchoir, who wear stubbies, blue singlets and Blundstone boots. While I'm sure the audience was relieved I'd finally stopped wittering at them, they must have been completely bewildered by my decision to close the show by rolling out what looked like a bunch of workmen I'd found backstage.

Some might say I didn't belong at the Opera House back then, but I disagree. What makes the building so special is that over fifty years it's evolved into being so much more than just an opera house. It's everybody's house.

— Kitty Flanagan is a multi-award-winning Australian comedian. She has written and starred in the award-winning ABC TV sitcom *FISK*. She's won a Logie for Most Popular Actress. She's had a best-selling book entitled *488 Rules for Life* for which she has won multiple awards and she sells out the biggest venues in the country.

BRIAN THOMSON

I remember walking to Bennelong Point and seeing the Opera House, now fully realised. As I left, I looked back at the building and decided to do everything possible to make those stages work.

Jane Harders and Peter Carroll in Sydney Theatre Company's *Chinchilla*, by Robert David MacDonald, directed by Rodney Fisher, Drama Theatre, 1981. Photo: Dennis Del Favero. Courtesy of Sydney Theatre Company.

I was studying architecture in Perth in 1963 when a tutor lent me 'Platforms and Plateaus', Jørn Utzon's article from *Zodiac 10* magazine in which he describes a transformative study trip to Mexico some years earlier. 'The platform as an architectural element,' Utzon wrote, 'is a fascinating feature.'

The following year, when I transferred to the University of NSW, the second thing I did after buying a pair of Beatle boots and tickets to all their stadium concerts was to go down to the Sydney Opera House site at Circular Quay. All that was there then was the podium, so I had the pleasure of watching the sails rise over time. My class was given a tour of the site, and that was when I met Utzon. He was a magnificent man, with such an air of confidence and grace. I was part of the protest marches when he resigned in 1966.

Over the next few years, I left architecture, moved to London and began designing for the stage. Jim Sharman and I were invited to create a production of *The Threepenny Opera* for the opening season of the Drama Theatre in 1973. On arrival back in Sydney, I remember walking to Bennelong Point and seeing the Opera House, now fully realised. As I left, I looked back at the building and decided to do everything possible to make those stages work.

From that point, I designed new productions of fifty shows at the Opera House, plays, musicals and operas plus a couple of Lord Mayor's parties outside. All this time, my career continued to shift from movies to opera to theatre. None of that was by design; it was just what happened.

Inside the Opera House, the Drama Theatre brought its own challenges but also some terrific solutions. As it did with *Festen*, in 2005, when I etched a line from a Leonard Cohen song, 'The Guests', into plywood as the curtain covering the front of the stage. I connected that line with the story of the play, a family get-together where everything went terribly wrong. Earlier that year, I had seen that song performed by ANOHNI in *Came So Far for Beauty*, a celebration of Cohen's music in the Concert Hall.

A different highlight was *The Portage to San Cristobal of AH*, in 1983, a play about finding Hitler up the Amazon, starring Barry Otto as the ageing Führer. The set was a reflection of the Drama Theatre, but the room was shown as it would look after it had been decayed or bombed, complete with a shattered version of John Coburn's *Curtain of the Moon*.

Another was *Macbeth*, in 1982, with John Bell and Robyn Nevin. The set was Uluru red, with horizonal panels that moved at any angle. When the forest comes to the castle, we had a giant green cloth emerge from the floor, the green contrasting with the red, which was visually staggering.

But there's one that stands out. On 10 November 1981, we opened a production called *Chinchilla: Figures in a Landscape with Ruins* by Robert David MacDonald. It was a play about the politics behind the scenes of Diaghilev's Ballets Russes, directed by Rodney Fisher with lighting by John Rayment.

I'd been working in film studios in London and was keen to see how an infinity cyclorama would work on stage. Every film studio had one, but it was rarer in the theatre. It meant that when you looked inside, you couldn't perceive distance.

In this production, the set was a vivid white wraparound cyclorama with a black beam across the proscenium that reinforced the challenging horizontality of the space. Towards the end, as the music swelled, Diaghilev was seated as clouds chased around the walls. Suddenly the music and cloud movement stopped and the actor, Peter Carroll, slumped in the chair. You know how it feels when you look up at a skyscraper and it looks like the building is moving against the clouds? That was the effect. It was a particularly physical feeling. I was using the horizontality of the room. I was determined to make everything at the Opera House work, almost in spite of itself. And that was a moment that really worked.

— Brian Thomson AM has been a designer for stage and screen since 1971, with his many honours including Helpmann, Tony and AFI awards. He has worked for all the major theatre companies in Australia as well as Broadway and West End on musicals, films and opera.

VICKI VAN HOUT

I let go of my preoccupations with mortality and committed to the underlying message of the work and my role within it.

First, a confession: until this appointment, I was deathly afraid of heights. So what the hell was I doing, dangling from a 2.7 tonne block of ice above Sydney Harbour on 14 January 2022? At fifty-four, I was becoming, you could say, well-seasoned for a physical performer. It felt like my shelf life was nearing its end. So, in the spirit of every other person suffering a mid-life crisis, I abandoned caution and threw myself at the chance for a place in the new production by Legs On The Wall, a show called *Thaw* that had been scheduled for the Sydney Festival. The company's artistic director, Josh Thomson, thankfully decided to go with this ol' broad from Dapto.

I quickly established a routine that began with a bicycle ride to the venue, parking conveniently at the racks outside Stage Door. My dressing room was tight but just right to quell my mounting excitement – also known as stage fright – before stepping onto the ice. I always managed a sneaky stretch, using the busy fixtures of that tiny cubicle to suitably contort my muscles in preparation for the ensuing physical onslaught.

As I emerged awkwardly from the labyrinthine backstage to the Forecourt, trussed up in layers of synthetic fabric to buffer me from the unforgiving surface of the ice, it was as if the Opera House was reassuring me, reaffirming her position in this endeavour, reminding me that she would stay at my side. A partner in crime, of sorts.

It took a slew of technical experts to suspend us beside the famous sails, from lifeguards poised at the shoreline, to crane operators and emergency crew on hand to assist me should I somehow lose consciousness mid-swing. My harness was checked with so many hands I lost count. Definitely more times than security at any airport.

I was up on the ice for a little under three hours each day. Because I was the first of three performers, the ice was fresh. It would speak to me in crackling sounds as it, too, settled and expanded in performance.

I apprehended the scale of the work anew each time I ascended. I let go of my preoccupations with mortality and committed to the underlying message of the work and my role within it. Each slowly melting block of ice, a sculpture that took two weeks to produce and as many years to design, represented the effects of global warming. My character became more sinister as the real estate I performed on shrunk. From a glamorous, though excessively consumerist solo

Following spread_ Vicki Van Hout in Legs On The Wall's *Thaw*, 2022. Co-presented by Sydney Opera House and Sydney Festival. Photo: Prudence Upton. Courtesy of Legs On The Wall.

traveller, docked at the most iconic Australian tourist destination, I was transformed into the figurehead of an unnamed, environmentally uncaring multinational conglomerate and the embodiment of a dying ecosystem. As a First Nations artist, I relished playing against type as the bad guy, the environmental nemesis, instead of an iteration of 'Mother Earth'. My favourite line – 'I am the face of progress!' – was delivered while smoking (and munching on) a cylindrical block of charcoal, only to let it dribble from my mouth and onto the ice, before I danced the black into its crevices and down its sides.

Many things travelled through my mind during the performance, including a memory of climbing the Harbour Bridge white-knuckled the previous summer, barely daring to look down, to the wonderment of watching birds flying past me at eye level, before returning to the overriding urgency of the environmentally charged *raison d'etre* of *Thaw*. As I was hoisted to the highest level, the Opera House became my guide, the host showing me the wonders of the harbour as Bennelong and Patyegarang would have done many years before. I was thankful it offered shelter for the audience from so many vantage points. From the midday sun, I thought I too would melt, or when the rain came and made me, and the ice, momentarily indivisible as (dripping) bodies of water.

This building has, over the years, been intrinsic to my career as an independent Indigenous artist. I remember thinking I was dreaming when, as a dancer with Bangarra, my body was buffed silver against a backdrop of smoke from forty-gallon drums filled with burning eucalyptus leaves as part of *Tubowgule* on the Forecourt, in the lead-up to the 2000 Olympic Games. I performed several solos as part of Blak revues in the Studio curated by NAISDA Dance College. As an independent choreographer, my collaborators and I performed a tongue-in-cheek a cappella 'Welcome to Country' dance in thongs, a traditional tap dance of sorts, on the Opera Theatre stage (breaking into the Playhouse to rehearse) for the Australian Dance Awards. Years later I performed on that same stage, then renamed the Joan Sutherland Theatre, as part of the *UnWrapped* initiative, to an empty seating bank, while the city was in lockdown.

For me, that performance of *Thaw* reaffirmed an ongoing relationship to a revered space, one that includes the ongoing perpetuation of Blakfella narratives and perspectives of which I am honoured to be included.

Each slowly melting block of ice, a sculpture that took two weeks to produce and as many years to design, represented the effects of global warming.

__ Vicki Van Hout is a Wiradjuri contemporary artist born on Tharawal country and residing on Gadigal land. She was the 2019 recipient of the Australia Council Award for Dance celebrating her work in the dance and Indigenous arts sectors as teacher, mentor, performer and performance maker.

DAVID McALLISTER

'You're never doing this again,' I thought, 'so just give it your all. Leave it all out there.'

David McAllister hangs up his shoes in 2001 after his
final performance as a dancer for The Australian Ballet.
Photo: Branco Gaica. Courtesy of The Australian Ballet.

In late 2000, I was appointed artistic director of The Australian Ballet, the company I had first joined in 1983. I had been a principal artist for eleven years, so at first I thought I would just stop dancing to focus on the new role. But Ross Stretton, the outgoing director, said I needed a farewell before taking the next step. He settled on the perfect setting: *Giselle* in the Opera Theatre the following year. That would be my final performance as a dancer.

Giselle had been the first professional performance I ever did, all the way back in 1982 on a regional tour. This time, in 2001, I was dancing Count Albrecht, the lead male role, and it was a magical moment of a circle being closed. And on that final night, a Saturday, 24 March, it felt amazing. All my family came, and I remember standing on the side of the stage, with my cloak and my sword, about to run down the ramp, and taking a few seconds to take stock of everything that was happening. 'You're never doing this again,' I thought, 'so just give it your all. Leave it all out there.' And it was the most extraordinary show. Everything happened without thinking. I guess I was in the zone. At the end, among all the streamers and flowers, I expected to be overcome with emotion and for there to be floods of tears. But as I stood there in the middle of the stage, looking out at my family and my friends, I just loved it. It was one of those nights where you think to yourself: this is it. I could die tonight and be happy.

The very next day, I got on a flight to San Francisco, the first stop of an eight-week overseas trip. Before taking over as artistic director, I wanted to visit ballet companies around the world, with a focus on directors who had been dancers in the companies they were directing. Then I came back, and a couple of weeks later I was the boss.

For me, the Opera House has always been there. I was once a ten-year-old in Perth, watching the opening of the House in 1973, wishing upon a star, and then there I was, doing my last show there almost thirty years later. There was something about being in that space that made these moments more elevated. If you're going to hang up your shoes, then you want to do it on one of the world's great stages.

It was one of those nights where you think to yourself: this is it. I could die tonight and be happy.

My first time working in the building was all the way back in 1983, not long after I had joined the company. We were doing *Spartacus* for The Australian Ballet's twenty-first anniversary, with Gary Norman in the lead role, and I remember feeling really excited when I turned up to work. For thirty-eight years after that, I had the honour of working continuously in the Opera House, first as a dancer and then as artistic director, and that first sense of occasion always remained with me. I know I'm not the only one who feels this way. It never loses its majesty.

___ David McAllister AC was artistic director of The Australian Ballet from 2001–2020. A graduate of The Australian Ballet School, he joined The Australian Ballet in 1983, was promoted to senior artist in 1986 and to principal artist in 1989.

Following spread_ David McAllister in *Giselle*, Drama Theatre, 2001. Photo: Branco Gaica. Courtesy of The Australian Ballet.

CASEY DONOVAN

I never thought I'd get
that far in a singing
contest, but there I was,
walking up those stairs,
walking the red carpet,
knowing nothing was ever
going to be the same.

My life changed at the Opera House, more than once. The first time was in 2003, when I took part in Young, Black & Deadly, the singing contest syndicated through Koori Radio. The final took place at the Playhouse, and that was also when I met Rhoda Roberts, the trailblazing producer who went on to be a massive influence in my career. Even then, a teenager who never dreamed of playing on a stage like that, I knew it was a magical place.

The next year, I was back, and the spotlight had grown. The *Australian Idol* grand final on 21 November 2004 was destined to be a turning point, no matter what happened and no matter who won. I was only sixteen, and I remember sitting in a stretched Porsche with Anthony Callea, the other finalist, as we made our way to the Opera House. I was feeling stressed about not wanting to put holes in the seats with my heels. I never thought I'd get that far in a singing contest, but there I was, walking up those stairs, walking the red carpet, knowing nothing was ever going to be the same.

I sang Tina Arena's 'Symphony of Life' with a massive chorus in front of a packed auditorium. Then came the moment. The announcement. Anthony and I were standing on stage, facing the hosts, and they said my name. After that, it was a whirlwind. I'd just won Australia's biggest national singing contest, the youngest winner, too, but in the seconds that followed I couldn't remember the words to the winner's single, 'Listen With Your Heart'. I had to ask Anthony how it began. Then I was whisked away to the media room, then to a party, then back to my hotel to hang out with my mates, then up first thing for more media, on and on it went.

It felt amazing to experience this huge moment in my life inside an Australian national treasure. The Opera House has been the backdrop to a lot of major events in my story. Looking back now, I feel like part of the furniture. I've seen the Opera House change over the years. I've hosted the Deadly Awards there, and sung on various occasions, including the Opera House's 40th birthday celebrations in 2013 and those television specials that bring in the new year. It's lovely to be invited back again and again, and I certainly have visions of *Idol* every time I walk into the building. The Opera House is a big part of my life. It holds a lot of joy.

__ Casey Donovan is a singer, songwriter, actress and author.

Following spread_ Casey Donovan reacts after being announced as the winner of *Australian Idol* in the Concert Hall on 21 November 2004. Photo: Andrew Meares. Courtesy of Fairfax Media.

RICHARD BONYNGE

I can still see the streamers
falling from the ceiling:
it was very moving. That
was the last time Joan did
a complete opera on stage.

For a time, in the late 1800s, Sydney was a good opera city. But from the turn of the century, and for some years afterwards, there was very little interest. Dame Nellie Melba had enjoyed success in Melbourne, but otherwise there was really nothing in Sydney until I came along with my wife, Joan Sutherland, as part of the JC Williamson touring company in 1965. We did eight shows a week for fourteen weeks and seven operas. We had a great chorus and great soloists.

When the season was over, we returned to England and Switzerland. There was a lot of talk in Sydney about that new building on the harbour, but I can't say we followed much of the conversation in any particular detail. We didn't really know what was going on with the Sydney Opera House. We were too busy performing, moving from country to country, and that took all our energies and all our thoughts. Eventually, Joan was asked to perform at the opening, but then the date changed; she had another engagement that couldn't be cancelled. That meant it wasn't until 1974 that we came home to work at the new Opera House in Sydney. The occasion was *The Tales of Hoffmann,* a big romantic production by Tito Capobianco.

Two years later, I started as music director of The Australian Opera, later renamed Opera Australia. I'm very proud of what we did together. We brought 18th and 19th century opera into the Opera House, big operas that had been neglected like *Alcina, Lucrezia Borgia, Les Huguenots, Lakmé* and *Lucia di Lammermoor,* of course. It's not up to me to say that this was a golden period for opera in Australia, but I felt that it was.

Joan was always happy to come to Sydney because it was her home. She also cared a lot about the opera company. Her performances were incredible and always sold out: people slept outside the Opera House just to get into her performances. It was the same all over the world. In New York, at the Metropolitan Opera, we had the freedom to do all sorts of material because they knew she would sell the house out. We worked together for a long time: I knew what she was capable of and I tried to help her to be the best she could possibly be. But I did that with all the singers. I didn't give her any special treatment; she didn't need it. She was a great artist and the public loved her.

Sometimes the performance itself becomes so strong and so powerful that it carries you away. As the conductor, though, you must keep ice in your head. After all, you're performing for a lot of people and it's not about how you feel but how they feel. You can't afford to get lost in

Following spread_ Curtain call of Dame Joan Sutherland's farewell performance, 1990. Photo: Don McMurdo, National Library of Australia, nla.obj-146354479.

the music, but at the same time, you have to feel it strongly. If you're not making people feel something, then you're not doing your job. You have to create a sense of magic in the theatre. You have to feel it and then project it.

These days, I don't listen to records much because I don't have the time. But when do I put on something, I'm still amazed when I listen to Joan's recordings. Sometimes I can't believe how she did it. Her voice was God-given. It was a great instrument, a beautiful instrument, but she also worked on her technique and that's why she had a long career. She not only had the voice, but she knew what she was doing with it. She was an incredible singer and always reliable.

We had so many memorable performances at the Opera House together. Like *Alcina* in February 1983: it was directed by Robert Helpmann, and even though I don't think he understood the opera well, he had the ability to make something just happen on stage. We'd done *Alcina* all over the world – at Covent Garden, La Fenice, in America – and this was the most beautiful of them all. It remains with me very strongly.

Even more memorable, but for different reasons, was Joan's final appearance on stage. It was a Wednesday, 2 October 1990, and I was conducting her in *Les Huguenots*, the 1836 opera by Meyerbeer. I don't think it was necessarily her best performance that night, but it was a wonderful opera and she loved it. The audience were lovely. They were encouraging, and it was a great pleasure because we were all like a family and I will never forget those years.

Everyone went out of their way to make it special. I can still see the streamers falling from the ceiling: it was very moving. That was the last time Joan did a complete opera on stage. She wasn't unhappy about that. She had been doing opera for forty-five years and had decided it was time. Why did she choose the Sydney Opera House to say farewell on that night? Sentimental reasons. This was our home. And in a way, it felt like our Opera House, too. She was very happy about doing her last one there.

— Richard Bonynge AC CBE has conducted in many of the
world's leading opera houses in a career that includes
multiple performances with his wife, the late Dame Joan
Sutherland. Born in Sydney, he was music director of the
Sutherland-Williamson Grand Opera Company in 1965,
artistic director of the Vancouver Opera from 1974–77 and
music director of The Australian Opera from 1976–86.

Dame Joan Sutherland as Alcina in the Opera Theatre,
later Joan Sutherland Theatre, in 1983. Photo: Don McMurdo.

FRANCES RINGS

For me, as a young Indigenous woman, part of a company that travelled the world, it was so good to be able to slow down and have that moment on stage with my peers, and just remember.

It felt like a cultural renaissance, particularly in Sydney, when the Olympics came around in the year 2000. Hundreds of Indigenous people from around Australia travelled to town for the opening ceremony. There was definitely a buzz. It felt like a snapshot in time: this is Indigenous Australia right now. These are the stories that are changing perceptions of who we are.

At Bangarra Dance Theatre, we had been travelling the world, but we could feel the momentum at home, too. With that came the fearless vision that Stephen Page had for the company and the work we were doing at the time. We performed at the opening ceremony and then we watched Cathy Freeman as she lit the cauldron, all these images being beamed across the world. And then we went straight from the Olympic Games – showing our art, our culture, our stories, our ancestry – to the Sydney Opera House to share our contemporary experience.

We were presenting a work called *Skin*, choreographed by Stephen Page as part of the Olympic Arts Festival, from 19 September 2000. There was a women's section, Shelter, and a men's section, Spear. It opened with a revered Torres Strait Islander leader and artist, Elma Kris, sitting on the stage, cradling a child (played by Hunter Page-Lochard and Rhimi Dean Johnson Page). I was a dancer on stage, performing in the women's section, and the part I remember is what happened after the dancing had stopped.

Archie Roach was appearing with us as a guest, along with other artists like Wayne Blair, who had just graduated from college. David Page did the score, Stephen Page did the choreography and Russell Page was performing. It was bliss to have the magic of those creatives in this space. How fortunate I was to be able to have that experience in my artistic DNA so that I can share that with others! When you look back at the legacy and history of Bangarra, that moment was a sweet spot, to have those artists come together, to tell that story in that iconic place at that time,

Following spread_ Peta Strachan, Frances Rings and Elma
Kris in Bangarra Dance Theatre's *Skin*, Drama Theatre, 2000.
Photograph: Michael Rayner. Courtesy of Bangarra Dance Theatre.

the Olympic Arts Festival, with the world looking at us, and having that responsibility to tell our stories.

At the end, as part of our curtain call, Archie sang 'Took the Children Away'. That song is an anthem for a reason. When Bangarra tells a story, we evoke a timeless space, a past and a present. You carry other people's stories, but that song is your own story, the story of your own grandmother, your own grandfather, a government policy that affected every Indigenous person in Australia. So that moment was about acknowledging, honouring and remembering those people but also knowing that they hold us up so we can tell our stories and carry them into the future. It was very emotional, a powerful and symbolically strong moment.

Normally we just come out and do our bows. We're exhausted, so we go off and do our thing, but this moment was sacred. It gave us the opportunity to sit together in this space while Archie sang his anthem. For me, as a young Indigenous woman, part of a company that travelled the world, it was so good to be able to slow down and have that moment on stage with my peers, and just remember.

Archie knew that song was important for a nation's healing. We talk about truth-telling, doing your bit to create change, to shift people's perceptions of Indigenous Australia, to promote healing and understanding. Every time he sang that song, you knew that was an important, pivotal moment. Not just for Bangarra but also for Australia.

There's something about a building and a space that adds layers to you as a person and as an artist. Being able to know that space already has an understanding of your DNA, that it hears the whispers of your stories, it understands you. The Opera House is a building, but it also contains the echoes of generations, especially with Bangarra and its dancers, and that makes it very special.

I have visceral reactions when I walk into the Opera House because of all the work I've performed in and created. Especially in the Drama Theatre; when I walk down that corridor, and down that passage, it floods back. But that curtain call after *Skin* was especially important because I could share it with my peers. It was a moment that invited the audience to come together and share in our healing. And that's rare to have as part of a performance. It's an important part of creating change.

The Opera House is a building, but it also contains the echoes of generations, especially with Bangarra and its dancers, and that makes it very special.

__ Frances Rings became artistic director of Bangarra Dance Theatre in 2023, having been associate artistic director since 2019. She has received multiple awards for her work, including six Helpmann Awards, a Deadly Award, an Australian Dance Award and a Green Room Award.

CARLOTTA

Oh my God, we're appearing at the Opera House. We're taking huge props into the Concert Hall. Is any of this going to work? Will the tickets even sell? It was a shock for everyone really.

Kings Cross was the Las Vegas of Australia. Even the strip clubs were glamorous. It had a seedy side, but Vegas did too. When I went overseas, all anyone wanted to talk about was Kings Cross, and it's definitely not like that anymore.

Les Girls was a restaurant in Kings Cross, owned by Sammy Lee and Reg Boom. It was a Sydney institution, along with some other clubs around the city like Chequers and the Latin Club, places where people like Sammy Davis Jr and Shirley Bassey turned up.

The cast of Les Girls on the steps of the Sydney Opera House
in 1974. Carlotta pictured back, centre. Photo: Neville Whitmarsh.
Courtesy of News Corporation Australia.

Les Girls, our variety show, emerged out of that scene. It was a Vegas-type showgirl show. We had a Judy Garland impersonator, showgirls and huge production numbers like they do in Las Vegas, and a lot of comedy, too. People wouldn't believe they were boys. It wasn't like impersonations today, where the performers only dress up at night. There was a fascination, more than anything else. People were just intrigued.

When we started, I thought it was a novelty. I didn't think it would last, but it just took off and now you turn on the TV and see footballers dressing up in drag. It was a great success, but it was also a learning curve every year. A choreographer gave me a good piece of advice when I was young. 'You're talented,' he said, 'but never believe your own publicity because there's always someone around the corner.' I've never forgotten that.

What put Les Girls on the map was a 1964 television documentary called *The Glittering Mile*. It was mostly about Kings Cross, but we featured in it, and from then on, our shows were packed.

In the early 70s, we moved to a big Greek club on Oxford Street, the Odeon. It was while we were there that we were asked to perform across town at the Sydney Opera House. We did two huge shows in the Concert Hall, on 11 and 12 July 1974, and both were absolutely packed. Presented by Les Girls, *10 Years in Revue* featured a cast that included Phaedra, Electra, Ayesha, Kali-Sue and Chanelle St Laurent.

I was Carlotta, the compere, and this was my opening line: 'Hands up those who've never been to Les Girls?' Most of the audience put their hands up. I asked where they were from, and it turned out that most of them had come from the other side of Sydney Harbour, over in the North Shore. 'So, you've never really crossed the bridge,' I said.

We were very nervous. *Oh my God, we're appearing at the Opera House. We're taking huge props into the Concert Hall. Is any of this going to work? Will the tickets even sell?* It was a shock for everyone really. At one point, we were in the Green Room and Joan Sutherland walked past with music sheets in her hand and the biggest cream bun I've ever seen in my life. I've always been a Joan Sutherland fan, so I was thrilled to bits. She was performing in *The Tales of Hoffmann*. A couple of us snuck into her dress rehearsal, which was fabulous.

I've appeared at other times at the Opera House, including in a Trevor Ashley variety gala, but that first night in the Concert Hall stands out above them all. You'll never see the likes of that again.

LES GIRLS

— Carol Spencer AM, or Carlotta, is an icon of the Australian cabaret industry. She began her career in the 1960s as one of the original members of Les Girls and went on to appear in a variety of television and stage roles. An inspiration for the film *The Adventures of Priscilla, Queen of the Desert*, she received widespread publicity in the early 1970s as a transgender woman, and in 2020 was named a member (AM) in the general division of the Order of Australia for significant service to the performing arts and to the LGBTIQ community.

The Les Girls program.

ROBYN NEVIN

And that is the grand
purpose of our Opera
House: to offer to the
public the playing out
of the full range of
human expression.

Robyn Nevin in the Sydney Theatre Company's *The Perfectionist*, by
David Williamson, directed by Rodney Fisher, Drama Theatre, 1982.
Photo: Dennis Del Favero. Courtesy of Sydney Theatre Company.

It was looking back, it was the moment of looking back. In the 1980s, I worked as an actress for the Sydney Theatre Company before I became its artistic director, and my memories of working inside the great building are vivid, particularly of New Year's Eve performances where we had long intervals to accommodate the audiences' fascination with the fireworks. But it was during a season of David Williamson's *The Perfectionist*, which opened on 20 July 1982, that offered The Moment.

After finishing a performance on the stage of the Drama Theatre, it was my habit to walk to my car, parked in those distant days inside the Royal Botanic Garden. Yes, amazingly we parked in an area just inside the gates to the garden designated as the domain of Governor Macquarie back in 1816. I walked from my dressing room out through the stage door and along the concourse under the massive concrete steps, emerging into the night air and turning right to walk along the sea wall to where my car waited inside the Governor's imposing gates. I would reverse my car from its romantic sea wall parking space, drive through the gates, across the Forecourt and out through the simple unguarded exit onto Macquarie Street and home to Paddington.

That was my nightly ritual. But one night, midway between the House and my car, I turned to look back. Why? I knew what was behind me: a massive monument to Art, a sculpture on the edge of our Sydney Harbour, my workplace. Perhaps it was the energy still pulsing after a performance that doesn't quieten for some time – the adrenalin keeps dancing within – so perhaps that energy, that restlessness, caused me to turn around. What I saw that night stayed with me, a vivid image that filled me with awe: the sky was bright, lit by a huge white moon and that moon shone onto the massive sails of Utzon's House so they gleamed.

Were they white, were they silver or were they black as in a Peter Kingston painting? The silhouette was dramatic. My response was dramatic. I was profoundly moved, stirred. It's a familiar feeling, it's what happens deep within when I'm moved by something; sadness, beauty, joy. It's a terribly hard emotion to describe and that's why we need poets and painters and composers and stories. But it's my sense that it's simultaneously a feeling of poignancy and a kind of ecstasy. They both hit at the same moment. That was my moment!

... the sky was bright, lit by a huge white moon and that moon shone onto the massive sails of Utzon's House so they gleamed.

No wonder we want more. No wonder we seek it in music and song and in stories. And that is the grand purpose of our Opera House: to offer to the public the playing out of the full range of human expression. I know why I paused and turned that night and each night after – because, aside from its beauty, the massive dark sculpture offered a meaning, a meaning particular to me, an actress fresh from the stage in my role as a storyteller. It's why that building exists. It's there to celebrate the performing arts, and I am a performing artist.

— Robyn Nevin AO has been a leading figure on Australian stage and screen for more than six decades. As well as leading roles for every major theatre company, and acclaimed performances on television and film, her credits as an administrator include associate director of the Melbourne Theatre Company, artistic director and CEO of the Queensland Theatre Company, and artistic director and CEO of the Sydney Theatre Company.

WILLIAM BARTON

The clapsticks used
in the performance
were made from old
and new floorboards of
the Concert Hall stage.
Holding those clapsticks
were the storytellers
of the next generation.

William Barton in the renewed Concert Hall in 2022, holding
clapsticks made from parts of the stage. Photo: Daniel Boud.
Following spread_ William Barton and Simone Young with
the Sydney Symphony Orchestra following the premiere of
Barton's new work, *Of the Earth*, to mark the opening of the
renewed Concert Hall. Photo: Daniel Boud.

I've played the Sydney Opera House Concert Hall countless times over the years. It's my second home. But the show that really resonates was one where I wasn't on stage at all. On 20 July 2022, I was watching from the stalls as the Sydney Symphony Orchestra, the Sydney Children's Choir and Gondwana Indigenous Children's Choir performed the world premiere of my new work, *Of the Earth*. These were the first sounds an audience was hearing inside the new Concert Hall after a long period of renovations, and those first sounds were coming from the pen of an Aboriginal composer. It was connecting back to Country, acknowledging our language and the landscape and finding symbolic gesture to move forward. It was a pivotal moment in my career.

Simone Young, the orchestra's chief conductor, had invited me to compose a new work that would open the new Concert Hall. The invitation had come as part of the Sydney Symphony Orchestra's *50 Fanfares* project, and I was one of fifty composers commissioned. For the reopening concert, the orchestra was going to play Mahler's Second Symphony, the *Resurrection*, so Simone gave me Mahler's large orchestra and choir to use for myself as well. The full toolkit.

Part of my process, when I write, involves a daily walk. I draw inspiration from the landscape around me. And when I worked on this project, I often walked past the Opera House to envisage my home in that building. It was my way of walking the land, a multi-layered journey of feeling and emotion. When I'm walking, I draw inspiration from the moment, but I also use the time to think about my Country and the journey I have taken. A hundred years ago, on the other side of the world, Mahler liked to go hiking on summer mornings before returning to work later in the day.

I was in Italy during the final months of completing *Of the Earth*, so took the opportunity to visit Mahler's hut in Attersee, Austria. He wrote about the landscape himself, so I came to connect with the space in my own way. The name of my work, *Of the Earth*, speaks in its own way to Mahler's song cycle, *Das Lied von der Erde*.

But for me, the piece I was writing encapsulated my journey from Kalkadungu Country in Queensland to the present day. There were melodies based on a Kalkadunga song I wrote when I was fifteen, a reference to 'Ave Maria', which my mother used to sing, and other elements that connected to my father's Country. All this came together in the Opera House that night as the passing of culture, inspired by Songlines, and ended with a promise to future generations about sustaining culture and language.

The clapsticks used in the performance were made from old and new floorboards of the Concert Hall stage. Holding those clapsticks were the storytellers of the next generation. At the end, when the kids walked out, that was the pivotal point of connection that took us back to Kalkadungu Country, together with the music I wrote when I was younger. That sense of unity and connection carried through the piece.

We held a smoking ceremony for the clapsticks before opening night. There's always so much effort and energy put into first performances, but that was an important part of the process. Members of the Indigenous choir gathered at the top of the stairs, outside the Opera House, for the ceremony. It was our own statement of resurrection: here were the clapsticks, made from the Opera House itself, being played by the children of the future.

On opening night, I could hear everything from my seat, especially the domino effect of the choir as the clapsticks rang out from one side of the hall to the other. From where I was sitting, the acoustics were amazing. But it wasn't about me. This was a shared experience. A shared moment of hope. It was our interpretation of the Australian landscape with a spirit and lullaby that has been with me from the start.

__ William Barton is an award-winning composer, multi-instrumentalist and vocalist, widely recognised as one of Australia's leading didgeridoo players and composers. A proud Kalkadunga man, he was the recipient of the Australia Council's Don Banks Music Award in 2021 for outstanding contribution to music, and in 2023 was named the Queensland Australian of the Year.

PAUL NUNNARI

It's about describing the atmosphere, as well as the context of the artists and the artwork. That way, it's a full palette of experience ...

Stephen McAuley, centre, leads the audio description
of the Lighting of the Sails for Vivid Sydney on the
Western Broadwalk in 2014. Photo: Daniel Boud.

It was 2013. Still the early days of Vivid Sydney. I was working for the Department of Premier and Cabinet, helping to coordinate major events, helping to improve accessibility. Destination NSW, the event owner, was looking for ways to make Vivid more inclusive. How can someone who is blind experience the light installations of Vivid, all of which are obviously very visual? One idea was to interpret these projects through audio descriptions, revealing what those installations look like. The lighting of the Opera House sails marked the start of festivities each night, activating the whole Vivid footprint across Circular Quay, so I thought it could be a good test. If we could make it work at the Opera House, that would set a precedent for similar projects elsewhere across town.

From my perspective, accessibility is not just about physical access – lifts and other infrastructure – but also about finding ways to make programs more inclusive from a sensory and cognitive point of view. The Opera House was one of the first major cultural institutions in Australia to introduce relaxed performances for neurodiverse audiences. It's a place where artists with disability are promoted not as a point of difference but as a point of strength.

After talking to Destination NSW, I reached out to Jenny Spinak, accessibility manager at the Opera House, and we talked about the potential. For this project, she thought of Stephen McAuley, an audio describer and tour guide. He's very passionate, enthusiastic and engaging. The best audio description is more than simply describing the sails from a visual perspective. It's about describing the atmosphere, as well as the context of the artists and the artwork. That way, it's a full palette of experience, and it's something that someone who is sighted can experience as well – a feature that quickly became clear.

We launched the trial in May 2014 on the Forecourt, offering audio description a few days a week for up to forty people each night. We set out chairs to make everyone comfortable, gave them headphones and then Stephen started to speak. To enhance the immersion even further, we passed around a 3D model of the Opera House so they could feel the curvature of the sails, as well as one of the tiles from the building.

On that first night, a remarkable thing happened. Visitors who had been walking past us stood with our guests, listening to Stephen talking, and before long it became this wonderfully inclusive event. The whole thing lasted about twenty minutes. There was an introduction, then the installation, with Stephen describing all the elements as the items were passed around, and then he took questions. People brought their families, and it was just beautiful, some of us looking up at the sails, all of us connected through that audio description offering. Everyone, whether they were blind or sighted, was sharing the experience in real time.

It was a hugely successful component of Vivid, so we kept it running for years afterwards. I use that first night as a case study for others in the community. You can see in the photos how engaged the participants were. This was something they never had the opportunity to do before. Every night was oversubscribed. We had nothing but positive feedback.

Sometimes you go to an event where you feel separated, as a person with disability, from the activity around you. If you're a wheelchair user like me, that might mean being put into a specific area for people with limited mobility, ensuring your experience takes place with only a small group of people. This moment at Vivid wasn't like that. It was fully inclusive. That's why I loved the general public stopping by to watch and to listen. That's what true immersion looks like: sharing an experience as a community, then celebrating and talking about it together.

— Paul Nunnari is director, inclusive infrastructure, placemaking and experience with the Department of Regional NSW. A paralympian, Guinness Record holder and theatre performer, he works to embed accessibility and inclusion across regional events including the Tamworth Country Music Festival, Deni Ute Muster and Parkes Elvis Festival.

JENNIE BEGG

Her Majesty Queen Elizabeth II and His Royal Highness
Prince Philip, Duke of Edinburgh, arriving for a performance
of *The Magic Flute*, 1973. Photo: Leo Davis.

A ghostly moon was leaving the sky when I woke for my afternoon shift on the morning of 22 October 1973. It was a cool seventeen degrees, with a light breeze, not the north-westerly gale that had dogged Saturday's official opening of the Sydney Opera House.

My duties that day had been to cover The Queen attending a performance of *The Magic Flute* in the newly opened building. I had just returned from seven years in London, where I had done my share of official gigs, from the opening of Parliament to royal garden parties to Wimbledon, opera and ballet. In Sydney, I was a sub-editor on *The Daily Telegraph*, but I doubled as its entertainment reporter, so this was just another day's work. Even the rolling series of strikes across Sydney seemed familiar after London's long, dark winter of industrial unrest.

All the official business had taken place two days earlier, but because of the Munich Olympic Games massacre and a recent warning by Prime Minister Gough Whitlam about domestic terrorism, police and sharpshooters were all over Sydney. As I mingled with society luminaries that night in their tuxedos, ball gowns and long white gloves, as well as a smattering of tiaras, I had no idea that this night would begin a connection that would change my life. My work, my play and even the lives of my future family – my husband, Adrian, and our two children – would be inextricably linked to this cement-and-tiles cultural icon for the next fifty years.

The first opera I had seen was *La Bohème*, staged by the touring Australian Elizabethan Theatre Trust in Newcastle, back in 1957. I was hooked. Since then, I had attended operas in London, Paris, Milan, Madrid and now Sydney. On my wall at home hung a commemorative lithograph from the first Sadler's Wells performance of *Don Giovanni* in its new home at the London Coliseum in 1968.

But none of that had prepared me for the Australian-produced and designed version of Mozart's masonic masterpiece, completed only three years after the first colonials had raised their flags in 1788. Conducted by Charles Mackerras, directed by John Copley and designed by John Stoddart, this *Magic Flute* even included a reference to Vegemite. Afterwards, The Queen and Duke of Edinburgh met the cast, including children dressed in kangaroo, koala, monkey and sheep costumes. What were they thinking? What did she think? I wish I had been close enough to hear the Duke of Edinburgh. He was never shy about such things.

Following spread_ Dame Joan Sutherland and Luciano Pavarotti in the Concert Hall, February 1983. Photo: Don McMurdo.

I remember being struck, that night, by the Opera House's concrete. Everywhere: above, below, inside, outside. And also by the number of stairs. The Queen was wearing a striking boadod tangorino gown and silver evening shoes, and I was amazed she did not slow as she climbed hundreds of stairs from foyer to theatre to backstage and back. There was no major news to report, but I quietly hoped that this *Magic Flute* would never be staged again.

Life went on. I married and had children. I joined the Sydney Philharmonia Choirs and sang in its symphonic and chamber choirs for fifteen years. I performed hundreds of times in the Concert Hall – 1988 was a particularly busy year, when celebrations rivalled the opening in 1973. The Olympic Arts Festival in 2000 was another memorable time. Bach, Beethoven, Mahler, Rachmaninov, Verdi, Berlioz, Orff, Walton, Vaughan Williams, Elgar, Janáček, Mendelssohn, Brahms, Mozart, Vivaldi, Tallis, Britten, Bernstein: all composers now part of my life.

On to the second generation. My son, aged two, at his first Babies Prom was photographed in the Studio, dwarfed by a double bass. He went on to sing in St Andrew's Cathedral Choir and also performed at the Opera House. He joined The Australian Opera Children's Chorus under Sean O'Dea and sang in several operas including *Tosca*, *The Magic Flute*, *Turandot* and *Carmen*. His sister, meanwhile, played viola in Suzuki concerts in the Concert Hall and later with the Sydney Youth Orchestra. She, too, joined the Children's Chorus and sang in *Voss*, *Werther*, *Mer de Glace*, Baz Luhrmann's *La Bohème* and a memorable *Der Rosenkavalier* conducted by Stuart Challender. They were as at home doing homework and practising music as they were eating dinner in the Green Room, chatting with Luciano Pavarotti or watching Joan Sutherland knit.

In 1999, I took a turn on stage as a singing extra in Verdi's *Don Carlo*. I had done my ACL in a skiing accident, so limped on stage, crutches in the wings, for the famous Auto-da-fé scene.

My husband loved ballet, so we enjoyed watching The Australian Ballet, as well as Bangarra and the Sydney Dance Company, plus Sydney Theatre Company performances at the House. During one Sydney Festival, I spent almost every night of January there, which is why Adrian called it my second home.

I remember Pavarotti singing with La Stupenda in 1983; seven years later, I sang with him in Verdi's *Requiem* as part of the 3000-strong World Festival Choir in Verona. Other memories crowd in: Nelson Mandela, Sammy Davis Jr, Gurrumul, the Dalai Lama, Hannah Gadsby, the Russian cellist Mstislav Rostropovich turning his chair around so those of us in the choir seats behind the orchestra could watch him play. I even slept overnight outside the doors after a Sydney Philharmonia Choirs performance to see Dame Joan's final performance in *Les Huguenots*.

In July 2022, I was devastated when COVID-19 forced me to miss the reopening of the Concert Hall with Simone Young and the Sydney Symphony Orchestra. But it felt both symbolic and also a perfect bookend to a relationship across half a century when I was able to join an outdoor community choir performance, *Big Heart Sing*, as the start of the Opera House's 50th anniversary celebrations in October. I can't sing as well as I once did, neither could I walk up and down all those steps as fast, but it was an amazingly satisfying, uplifting celebration.

This was always a house for the people, for the community, not just performers. In my earliest memory of the building, my father bought tickets in the Opera House lottery, part of the fundraising efforts to pay for its construction. In 2014, the Opera House conducted another fundraiser, this time selling tiles from the sails during its Decade of Renewal – and my husband bought one for my seventieth birthday. 'The Sydney Opera House is a masterpiece that belongs to all Australians,' the promotional material said. My tile, a digital version of the real thing, is number A02 W.15.24. It has a wonderful view from one of the great wonders of the world.

— After a cadetship on the *Newcastle Morning Herald*, Jennie Begg worked on the *Richmond and Twickenham Times*, then various papers on Fleet Street. Back in Australia she subbed on *The Daily Telegraph*, *The Australian* and *The Australian Financial Review* and managed AMP's financial communications. She was also a chorister at St James King Street and Christ Church St Laurence, Sydney, and sang in Sydney Philharmonia Choirs for fifteen years. She was a board member at SPC and a founding board member of St Andrew's Music Festival, Sydney.

SYLVIE GUILLEM

In September 2000, Sydney was the centre of the world. My husband and I had been planning to visit for the Olympic Games anyway, so when I received an invitation to perform at the Sydney Opera House, it felt very lucky.

When we arrived, we felt so much joy and positive energy. It was contagious. It seemed that everything and everybody were shining. The atmosphere across the city was electric. This excitement accompanied the shock, the wonder – the *émerveillement* – of finally seeing the Opera House in real life, that amazing gift to the world and its people. It was the wonder of having encountered true beauty. A gift from the mind of a genius and poet. A majestic offering, proof of what human beings can do at their best. A tribute to nature, movement and light.

I was there for *Boléro*, Maurice Béjart's production, for the Olympic Arts Festival, and it was like a dream. Like the other people around, I was euphoric. That unique building was the first thing I wanted to see. We looked at it, scanning it from every angle; we walked around it, we went on it, we took the boat to see it from all possible angles. It was as though I wanted to print it forever on my memory.

After that performance, I came back to Sydney regularly: for *Sacred Monsters*, *Push*, *6000 Miles Away*, before ending in 2015 with *Life in Progress*. That was a farewell tour that ended in Tokyo but also included Australia. I just had to go to Sydney as well.

When you're at the beginning of a career, everything feels like it's going to last forever. It's all happening so fast. You know that eventually it will end, so you go on enjoying most of it. But when you decide to bring things to a close, your relationship to time and everything else changes. Each gesture, every ritual or preparation, you're doing it at that particular place for the last time. And it is in full consciousness and sadness that you're methodically leaving a whole life behind.

On 25 August 2015, while preparing for my last show in the Opera House, I took a picture of my dressing room, a childish way to say goodbye to one intimate place that had been a witness to all my fears and happiness. There are some places I came back to regularly, places that are dear to my heart, and the Opera House has definitely been one of them. It was the kind of place you dream about.

__ Sylvie Guillem has performed all the leading roles of classical ballet with the world's foremost companies including The Royal Ballet, Paris Opera Ballet, the Mariinsky, American Ballet Theatre and La Scala. She began her career with the Paris Opera Ballet in 1981 as a member of the company's corps de ballet before becoming the youngest ever dancer promoted to the rank of étoile by Rudolf Nureyev at the age of nineteen. She later became a principal guest artist at The Royal Ballet then an independent contemporary dancer as an associate artist of the Sadler's Wells Theatre in London.

Following spread_ Sylvie Guillem in *Life in Progress*, Drama Theatre, 2015. Photo: Bill Cooper/ArenaPAL.

A gift from the mind
of a genius and poet.
A majestic offering,
proof of what human
beings can do at their
best. A tribute to nature,
movement and light.

RHODA ROBERTS

Cultural knowledge-holders were passing away. We started to ask how we could be more involved in the community because, like so many other people, we didn't want to be the generation that lost its Songlines.

Work by the late Kimberley artist Yorna 'Donny' Woolagoodja in *Songlines*, the first
Indigenous Lighting of the Sails, as part of Vivid Sydney in 2016. Photo: Daniel Boud.

The world was shifting. We were being heard and we were being seen. It wasn't necessarily political. We were just there, doing what we had always done.

It was late on the night of 27 May 2016, and I was at the Overseas Passenger Terminal, across the water from the Opera House, for the launch of *Songlines*. This first Indigenous Lighting of the Sails was an animation that featured the work of six artists from across the country. I remember crying from the emotion of it all.

The visibility of that moment – matching an iconic building with iconic art – was incredible. It went global. Opera House staff were still responding to requests for more information about the artists a year later. That sort of enthusiasm led to a project called *Badu Gili*, where we lit the eastern Bennelong sails 365 days a year. *Badu Gili* had come about from that earlier exposure, which meant that anyone could see that Aboriginal culture was as alive and relevant now as it was prior to colonisation.

I had started at the Opera House four years earlier as Head of Indigenous Programming, now Head of First Nations Programming. It was the first position of its kind in Australia at the time. We talked about enabling opportunities for our creative sector and for people to develop their skills. We were engaging with First Nations artists and the Australian community overall. It felt like the train had left the platform.

We'd been hearing for a long time that Songlines were disappearing across the country. Cultural knowledge-holders were passing away. We started to ask how we could be more involved in the community because, like so many other people, we didn't want to be the generation that lost its Songlines. That was the idea behind Dance Rites, a national First Nations dance competition launched in 2015 to share cultural knowledge from one generation to the next. That festival was a healing process for everyone. We were providing a platform for stories and re-creating transmission of culture. It was also wonderful, joyous fun.

I have so many Opera House memories, hundreds of them, but that night in 2016, when we launched *Songlines*, was the most defining of them all. It was about the acceptance of our art on this Australian icon. Here was the Opera House, representing the horizons of our country, showing how we were all connected.

It was the right time, too. We couldn't have done it ten years earlier. Our nation had changed.

Some of the artists were there. One of them had passed, so her family had come down from Arnhem Land for the event. Another artist, a man I had worked with for the Sydney Olympics, was so excited about coming to Sydney but he couldn't make it because he'd been hospitalised. Instead, he watched on a screen from his hospital bed with a little package of goodies that we'd sent. When I called, he told me it was better to watch from there because it was too cold in Sydney at that time of year. When I thanked him, he said that wasn't necessary, but I was just thinking how fortunate I was to be able to work in the arts with these Senior Custodians who had given me so much trust in their work. There were elements that were really quite sacred, but he allowed me to experiment because he knew I'd do the right thing. That was a wonderful gesture from a gentleman of his age and wisdom.

The *Songlines* project itself was quite innovative, so I was grateful to the artists for allowing us to take elements of their work and animate it on the Opera House. There was a huge amount of trust by the artists in the technology, but it meant we were able to show people this incredible diversity of art.

Everything is interconnected. We're using a new medium and new technology, but really, we're doing the same sort of thing. What resonated for me then, and now, was the knowledge that there always was Aboriginal art around the rocks or the escarpment around Farm Cove. We were doing what our ancestors had done.

— Rhoda Roberts AO is a curator, actor, producer, writer and festival director. Her many leadership roles include head of First Nations programming at the Sydney Opera House, festival director of the Boomerang Festival/Bluesfest, festival curator of the Parrtjima Festival, creative director First Nations programming for Northern Rivers Performing Arts and founding artistic director of the Festival of the Dreaming.

JIMMY BARNES

For a second, I can hear
the screams of my young
friends, high and piercing,
as we run wild and free
down the crumbling streets
of my old neighbourhood.

Billy Connolly at the Opera House in 1987. Photo: Don McMurdo.

As I come to rest in my seat at the Sydney Opera House, I am surrounded by sounds that pull me back to my youth. Accents I heard as a boy are drifting around me like songs. Not being sung on the stage but by the patrons who wander in hoping for a perfect place to see the show. Tartan scarfs, tied around the necks of grey-haired gentlemen who stand with arms spread defiantly across the aisle, clearing a path for their tight-lipped wives who mill slowly past in search of their seats. In the row behind me a trembling hand reaches for a hip flask deep in the pocket of an ill-fitting suit. Slowly the audience find their places and a hush of anticipation descends. This isn't just a show. This is a chance to see our lives re-enacted and reimagined in front of us.

It seems strange; as if my past, my present and my future have all come crashing together in this moment. If I close my eyes, I can smell the streets of Glasgow. Smoke rising from the chimneys that top the neat rows of tenements lining the filthy streets. The smog, an intoxicating blend of fumes from the factories mixed with the smell of salt from the Irish Sea, fills my lungs. For a second, I can hear the screams of my young friends, high and piercing, as we run wild and free down the crumbling streets of my old neighbourhood.

In those days, I dreamed of being old enough to run away. Away from the cold. Away from the rain. Away from the pain that I felt deep in my heart. Now here I was – as far away from those streets as I could possibly get but being drawn back gently. Back to my first home. A home that gave most of the people in this room, and the man we'd all come to see, a start in life. He would tell stories drawn from those streets we walked as children. Tell tales inspired by characters who walked beside us and behind us. Stories that allowed us to laugh at everything that hadn't killed us. My father drank at the same bars as this man and most of the people who sat here with me shared the same deep connection. I felt warm inside. I had made my way back home, but this time, with Billy Connolly's help, we would all find it funny.

The Opera House has always felt like a place of hope for me. When I first moved to Sydney, I drove over the bridge and daydreamed about one day singing on its stage. In 1997, fourteen years after Cold Chisel had performed The Last Stand – a series of concerts that ended a decade of dreams – we decided that our wounds had healed enough to get back together and continue the work we'd started back in 1973. The Opera House was where we came. In bright neon rooms deep below the Concert Hall, we rehearsed secretly day and night until we rekindled the fire that burned between us. After a month, we said goodbye to our sanctuary and unleashed ourselves on the world. Recharged and ready to rock, we commenced The Last Wave of Summer Tour. The backdrop for that tour was an enormous steel wave that curled over the stage. Maybe we chose it as a reminder of the sails that curl above the place where the five of us reignited our spark.

The Opera House, a place of beginnings for so many, has also always been somewhere you can lay things to rest. As I walk up those steps that lead away from the harbour toward the Concert Hall, I remember so many firsts and lasts. Little Stevie Wright's bloodcurdling scream as he sang 'Come on babe, you know there ain't no time to mess around', proudly fighting his demons on those steps. The whole country watching and cheering him on. Willing him to win a battle that was already lost. The ghosts of the thousands of people who watched Crowded House sing 'Better Be Home Soon' somewhere between the ocean and the silhouettes of the sails as the sun slowly set on Sydney Harbour. Now, in 2015, here I was again. Back to see Billy Connolly do his final tour and transport me into my childhood one more time in this special place where people have been coming and going for over 60,000 years.

Billy waltzed on to stage like a swashbuckling pirate. Moving from one side to the other. Riding the rapturous applause of the adoring crowd like it was a wave. These were his people. My people. He moved with the swagger of a man completely comfortable in his surroundings. Tonight, we were all going back home. 'Good evenin' everybody!'

— Jimmy Barnes is a Scottish-born singer-songwriter who grew up in Adelaide. As a solo performer and lead singer of Cold Chisel, he went on to become one of the most successful artists in Australian music history, selling more than twelve million albums and being inducted twice into the ARIA Hall of Fame. He is the best-selling author of the childhood memoir *Working Class Boy*, and its sequel, *Working Class Man*.

EDO DE WAART

The scale of this
achievement will be
recognised more and
more in the years ahead ...

I've worked in the great performance halls around the world, so the question was always there: how did this one compare? As a building, the Sydney Opera House has always been incredible. It looks unbelievable, especially when you have the opportunity to approach it from the water. I remember first seeing it from a hotel room in The Rocks. I opened the curtain from a switch next to the bed and there in front of me, across the water, was the Opera House. You couldn't make anything more attractive.

But in 1993, when I first took the stage as the Sydney Symphony Orchestra's new chief conductor, I realised the acoustics were less than ideal. No concert hall in the world has a dome like that above the stage, and that was where all the sound just disappeared. Those rings above the stage did nothing either. I told people what I thought, how it felt like there was like a curtain between the stage and the audience, and those comments made an impact. I wasn't trying to be political, but those comments made headlines around the world.

No one was really talking about this issue at the time. It sounded okay from the stage, but that's not always a good thing. It doesn't necessarily translate into what the audience hears. One of the most impressive concert halls in the world is the Concertgebouw in Amsterdam: when you stand on the conductor's podium, it can sound quite horrible, but when you walk into the hall there's this glorious sound. That's what we wanted to experience in Sydney.

I was the Sydney Symphony Orchestra's chief conductor between 1993 and 2003. It takes time, with an orchestra, to get used to each other. And it takes some years to hear the result. By the time Sydney hosted the Olympics, we were doing some amazing things together, and there's one that I remember vividly: the cycle of Wagner's *Ring* operas that ended in the Concert Hall with *Götterdämmerung (Twilight of the Gods)*, as part of the Olympic Arts Festival on 5 and 8 September 2000. We had performed *Das Rheingold* in 1995 and *Die Walküre* two years later, so this was a wonderful occasion. We got the most out of the hall that day, with music that was so full and so rich. We also appeared in a very different stage during that festival: a 20,000-seat venue called the Sydney SuperDome. That was where we played Mahler's Eighth, the symphony of a thousand, with almost a thousand people on stage.

I left Sydney in 2003 and have returned regularly since then. When I came back in the second half of 2022 to conduct the orchestra with South Korean pianist Yeol Eum Son, I couldn't believe my ears. The acoustics of the Concert Hall had been enhanced enormously. I went out into the hall to listen, and the difference was unbelievable. The scale of this achievement will be recognised more and more in the years ahead, not just when the Sydney Symphony Orchestra performs but when foreign orchestras come through, too. That's usually when halls become famous, when people want to come to Sydney to play and audiences want to come to Sydney to listen. That Concert Hall is now in line with what a great country deserves. The acoustics are so much better. Those changes were worth every penny.

___ Edo de Waart was chief conductor and artistic director of the Sydney Symphony Orchestra from 1993 to 2003.

SARAH BLASKO

They all beamed with pride, tears in their eyes, holding me, reminding me that I'd dreamed of singing with an orchestra since I was a child …

In 2013, when I performed my fourth album, *I Awake*, in full, with my band and a forty-piece orchestra over two nights, it was the first time I'd played my very own headline show in the Concert Hall. I'd performed in the Studio, written music for Bell Shakespeare's *Hamlet*, which we performed in the Drama Theatre, and been part of ensemble performances in the Joan Sutherland Theatre and on the Forecourt, but nothing could have prepared me for how significant a moment it would be to perform my own show in the Concert Hall.

I was going through some heartbreak at the time and was oblivious to the magnitude of this moment in my life and career as the concerts drew nearer. I was just focused on getting through, completely consumed by many of the external pressures involved in delivering a show like that. This was the first occasion an Opera House show was going to be livestreamed, so the pressure was on. Beyond that, performing with an orchestra for the first time on stage, and with a different ensemble in each city of the tour, meant we had to perform the entire set twice on the show day. This was starting to take a toll on my voice in the lead-up to the Sydney shows. I remember getting some acupuncture, drinking all manner of concoctions and seeing an osteopath friend to do whatever I could to heal my voice in time. She cracked my spine and told me that she'd done this for opera singers – perfect!

Following spread_ Sarah Blasko performing *I Awake* on the Concert Hall stage, 2013. Photo: Daniel Boud.

I'd done all I could possibly do to prepare, and then the day of the first show arrived. That's when it hit me. When I saw the faces of my closest friends, my bandmates and the people I'd been working with for ten years, I realised this was a huge, full-circle moment – not just for me, but for all of us. It hit me in that moment that they shared this triumph, this achievement as their own. And it was that which ultimately made it so important and so memorable a show for me. It also helped take some of the nerves away.

They all beamed with pride, tears in their eyes, holding me, reminding me that I'd dreamed of singing with an orchestra since I was a child, of the days we'd worked crap jobs together and all I could talk about was singing, how far I'd come from that first show they'd seen me do when they were the only people in the audience in this very same city, and look at us now! The flowers arrived, cards and congratulations, and they woke me up. They made me realise this was a moment worth celebrating at a time in my career and my life when I was focused either on what was ahead or the hurt that had consumed me. It was beautiful and unexpected.

The shows felt magnificent and I'm still so proud of them. After the second show, as I stood there in that beautiful, big Opera House Green Room, I cut into the cake my friend had made for me – he'd photoshopped my head next to the Opera House and printed it on the fondant; it was priceless – and was forced into a speech, of sorts. I raised my glass and looked around that room to everyone around me who had carried me to that moment.

_ Sarah Blasko is a widely acclaimed singer and songwriter, based in Sydney. A three-time ARIA award winner, she has released six solo albums and two with her trio Seeker Lover Keeper.

A celebratory cake for Sarah Blasko in the Green Room. Photo: Ben Fletcher.

DEBORAH MAILMAN

A massive storm. Rain across Sydney Harbour. The Harbour Bridge lit up, the sails of the Opera House above me and Barrie Kosky, in a fez, to my right. It was all very weird. There was a camera in my face and an earpiece in my ear and then I heard my name and Barrie came over to present me with an award and I was on TV and I'd won.

That was 7 November 1998. It was my most memorable night at the Opera House, but it wasn't my first experience of the building. That happened the previous year, when I arrived for the Sydney premiere of *7 Stages of Grieving*, the one-woman play I had created with Wesley Enoch. That was a very personal work for us. It had been in development for several years, moving gradually from a twenty-minute piece in Brisbane to the hour-long show we brought to Sydney. To have the opportunity to present it at the Opera House was pretty amazing. It was like we'd arrived. As a young actor, trying to find her feet in the industry, that was everything to me. We toured that show across the country. That was one of our intentions: that it would have a place and a life beyond us.

I remember turning up for the premiere and seeing the sails and not quite believing I was about to perform at the Opera House. Until then, all my work had been in Brisbane, so this felt very new. Simply walking up to the building felt breathtaking, and that feeling carried over to every time I performed at the Opera House. There's something magical about walking across the Forecourt then going under the stairs and checking in at stage door and passing through the Green Room and into the guts of everything and seeing everyone going about their daily work.

It becomes a home away from home, the back corridors and theatres. Those feelings of wonder also mix with the working reality of being. There are a lot of pinch-me moments in the Opera House, but there's also the reality of performing on stage. That sense of awe might be always there – it's one of the most beautiful places to perform, a real privilege – but at the end of the day, there's a job to be done.

That's how it felt when we worked on Barrie Kosky's production of *King Lear* in 1998 for Bell Shakespeare. The show was being presented downstairs in the Playhouse. John Bell was Lear. I was Cordelia. After the bow that night, when everything started to happen, I was still a bit dazed: it was a Kosky production, so you're going a hundred miles an hour. A few weeks earlier, after opening night, Bryce Hallett had written in *The Sydney Morning Herald* about Barrie's 'untamed, animalistic force', and it was true. He doesn't do anything half-arsed.

Someone pulled me off stage and Barrie was with me as we walked through the stage door into the night. I looked up to the sky and the huge electrical storm. We stood next to the Opera House, where a live feed had been set up to the AFI awards (now the AACTA awards). I listened through an earpiece, still in costume and full make-up from *King Lear*, and that was how I found out I'd won my very first AFI award for *Radiance*, the film by Rachel Perkins. The storm was still blowing when Barrie handed me the award. It was just a crazy, singular moment.

__ Deborah Mailman AM is an Australian actor. She has worked extensively in theatre, television and film, and received multiple honours for her performances, including Helpmann, AACTA, Logie, AFI and Deadly awards. She joined the Sydney Opera House Trust in February 2015.

Following spread_ Deborah Mailman in Bell Shakespeare's *King Lear*, Playhouse, 1998. Photo: Jeff Busby. Courtesy of Bell Shakespeare.

LYNDON TERRACINI

I remember thinking:
'Woah, now that's what
it's supposed to sound
like.' That concert left a
huge impression on me.

Bob Dylan. Courtesy Frontier Touring.
Following spread_ A scene from Opera Australia's
Rigoletto, Joan Sutherland Theatre, 2018. Photo:
Prudence Upton. Courtesy of Opera Australia.

The first performance I saw at the Sydney Opera House featured Birgit Nilsson, the famous Wagnerian soprano. Somehow I had a ticket to the opening gala in 1973 – a great seat, too. It was the most extraordinary thing I've ever heard. I remember thinking: 'Woah, now that's what it's supposed to sound like.' That concert left a huge impression on me.

But it wasn't my first experience of the Opera House. I remember driving across the Harbour Bridge in my battered Volkswagen, a car with rusty floors and not particularly good brakes, on my way to the NSW State Conservatorium, and looking down at that site where it was being built. I was at opera school, so I sang in some of the early test performances before the building opened – operas by Australian composers, James Penberthy's *Dalgerie* and Larry Sitsky's *The Fall of the House of Usher* – then turned up to rehearsals for *War and Peace*, the Prokofiev opera to be performed on opening night. It felt like every man and his dog was there, but it felt like nobody could read music and everyone was spending an hour on every two bars. I went to one rehearsal and never returned.

But I did make it to the first variety concert. I sang in a duet with Rolf Harris, and it was completely politically incorrect. Harris even taught me to play the didgeridoo, which is a pretty strange memory. Soon enough I found myself returning every week, doing backing vocals for singers like Helen Reddy and Olivia Newton-John. That was when Harry M Miller was presenting *Sunday Night at the Opera House*, live on Channel Nine.

Much later, when I was artistic director of Opera Australia, we performed more than 600 shows a year around the country, many of those taking place at the Opera House. If you asked me to name highlights, I might single out Jonas Kaufmann singing *Parsifal*; the digital-set productions, especially *Il Trovatore* in 2022; and all the phenomenal singers and conductors we worked alongside over the years, people like Andrea Battistoni, who was known as being the youngest conductor to work at Teatro alla Scala. Watching him in the pit was like watching Maradona play soccer. He did things other human beings just couldn't do.

But it's hard to go past what happened in August 2018 when I ended up giving Bob Dylan a singing lesson inside an empty theatre. We had sent him an invitation to *Rigoletto* via one of his band members. Right on the bell, Dylan made his way into the Joan Sutherland Theatre, wearing a hoodie. I suspect he thought the hoodie would make him anonymous, but no one else in the theatre was wearing one, so it probably had the opposite effect.

Renato Palumbo was conducting, and it was a terrific performance. The audience went bananas. After the show had finished, we stayed in our seats and had a long chat. Dylan was really interested in the art of singing without a microphone, so I showed him how it worked. It basically turned into a singing lesson: I showed him a few exercises, including one that lowered the larynx and made the voice more resonant. He did it a few times and couldn't believe the result. He was really impressed. 'Your voice is an instrument,' I said. 'You've got to allow it to speak. You're doing everything you possibly can to stop it speaking.'

The head usher could see what was happening and left us to do our thing. We ended up sitting there for about half an hour. It was fantastic. You could argue that Dylan changed the world, certainly for an entire generation.

The next night, Palumbo and I went to see Dylan in concert at the Enmore Theatre. Was there any difference in the sound of his voice? Not really. But it was still an extraordinary experience.

___ Lyndon Terracini AM, the former artistic director of Opera Australia, Queensland Music Festival and Brisbane Festival, has enjoyed a highly successful international opera career as well as a successful career as an actor, director and writer. In 2018 he was awarded one of the highest civilian honours in Italy, Commander of the Order of the Star of Italy (Commendatore dell'Ordine della Stella d'Italia).

PETER GILMORE

It was exhilarating and incredibly special to hear this piece of music that had been sung by the man himself, Bennelong.

Eric Avery and Clarence Slockee performing a song by Bennelong
at the Bennelong restaurant opening, 2015. Photo: Daniel Boud.

On 30 June 2015, we celebrated the opening night of Bennelong restaurant under my direction. The responsibility and privilege of running the premier dining space at the Opera House felt immense, exciting and also a little overwhelming. I am a Sydney-born chef, this is my home, and the Opera House is the architectural symbol of Australia.

In planning our new menu, I wanted to highlight the finest produce our land and oceans provide. A menu to represent our multicultural society in both technique and influence. And, importantly, a menu that would represent the cultural significance of the Opera House site. Bennelong Point was originally a meeting and gathering place to share food and stories for the Gadigal of the Eora Nation. This history makes the site of Bennelong restaurant more meaningful.

The first night for Bennelong was a cocktail party for 200 guests. The menu included Sydney rock oysters, yabby pikelets with lemon jam, sashimi of coral trout and tartlet of native muntries and young peas among other offerings. Dessert canapes included what would become my infamous take on the cherry jam lamington. The night began and guests started arriving. I felt the expectation in the room. The Fink family had just spent a significant amount of money renovating the dining room and rebuilding the kitchen. Everything was primed for a new era at the Bennelong restaurant.

A stage had been set up at the top of the dining room, where the glass meets the city views. After the Welcome to Country, two performers, Eric Avery and Clarence Slockee, both First Nations men, stepped up to the stage. Eric introduced the song they were about to perform: a traditional song by Bennelong. The score of the song had been written down after Bennelong and his young friend Yemmerrawanne performed it in London in 1793, the first time an Aboriginal and Torres Strait Islander song had been heard in Europe.

… the Opera House felt immense, exciting and also a little overwhelming.

On this night, more than two centuries later, at the new Bennelong restaurant, Clarence sang while Eric accompanied him on the violin. Their performance sent shivers down my spine. It was exhilarating and incredibly special to hear this piece of music that had been sung by the man himself, Bennelong. It made me appreciate, even more, the significance of this cultural site and its long history, both in a traditional and modern sense. The blending of culture within the performance, the traditional voice and the accompaniment of the violin, felt like time and place had merged into something spiritual. It was a moment I will never forget.

— Peter Gilmore is the executive chef at Bennelong at the Sydney Opera House and Quay Restaurant across the harbour in The Rocks. He is one of Australia's most awarded chefs, having been awarded Three Chefs Hats for an unprecedented nineteen consecutive years and named Restaurant of the Year six times in *The Sydney Morning Herald's Good Food Guide*. Quay was listed for five years on the World's 50 Best Restaurants list and held the title of Best Restaurant in Australasia for three of those years.

MAINA GIELGUD

My office was a dressing room overlooking the harbour. To sit in my own cabin on a ship of this kind was as calming as it was unique.

My love affair with the Sydney Opera House blossomed, then grew, then deepened during my fourteen years at the helm of The Australian Ballet. But the roots of this relationship began earlier, back in 1974, when I appeared as a guest artist with the same company.

My memory box is full of souvenirs. But first, let me take issue with those who point to mistakes. 'The stage is too small,' they said. 'There's no wing space,' they said. 'It's too cramped,' they said. I opposed these people with vehemence at the time, and I still do. As a dancer, as a coach, as a director, the atmosphere of a theatre venue, the connection between artist and audience, is by far the most important part of a performance hall. And the atmosphere of the Opera House has always been without peer.

In November and December 1974, when I appeared as the female lead in John Cranko's production of *Romeo and Juliet*, this atmosphere was particularly potent. Juliet is a fabulous role. It's a dancer's dream, neither tiring nor technically difficult, but everything comes together to bring the story alive, reaching out to touch every member of the audience. There was a bond that night between stage and audience, as sharp at the start as it was in the potion scene, when Juliet sits immobile on her bed, debating within herself whether she has the courage to drink from the vial from Friar Lawrence. I don't think I've felt that feeling of connection before or since.

Other incredible moments were still to come. Later that year, for example, I witnessed the Stuttgart Ballet's performance of Glen Tetley's *Voluntaries* featuring the original creators of the roles: Marcia Haydée, Birgit Keil, Richard Cragun and others. I had flown from Melbourne with Gary Norman, the Australian dancer, especially to see it. Our seats were quite a way back in the auditorium, but that performance was one of the most spiritual theatre experiences I have witnessed. At the end, Gary and I were speechless.

In 1983, when I was appointed artistic director of The Australian Ballet, I spent four months of every year in Sydney, all but living in the Opera House. Every day, coming into work, I marvelled at the sight of that architectural masterpiece and swore to myself I would never take it for granted. My office was a dressing room overlooking the harbour. To sit in my own cabin on a ship of this kind was as calming as it was unique. This was the room where casting decisions were confirmed, last-minute emergencies handled, conversations held with dancers, promotions made, as well as the endless discussions with general managers about

Following spread_ Maina Gielgud in rehearsal with dancers from The Australian Ballet. Photo: Jeff Busby. Courtesy of The Australian Ballet.

Above_ Maina Gielgud as Juliet in The Australian Ballet production of John Cranko's *Romeo and Juliet*, Opera Theatre, 1974. Photo: Walter Stringer, National Library of Australia, nla.obj-146911747.

tours and repertoire and so much more. But it was also a dressing room, so it was also where I put my hair in electric curlers after late rehearsals and dressed up for performances and receptions.

We enjoyed fleeting, memorable visits by artists like Ekaterina Maximova, Alessandra Ferri and Alexander Kølpin. The visit of the latter, from The Royal Danish Ballet, ended prematurely when he was injured in his solo during the balcony scene of another *Romeo and Juliet*. Seated in my usual place, I almost leapt to the stage as he fell.

How many times did I sit in those red seats in the stalls, not just for performances, but coaching and watching rehearsals? How many generations of dancers, working on such a multitude of roles in such diverse works, by some of the greatest choreographers of the 20th century as well as the big classics? A friend once told me that my time at the Opera House was like living in a fairyland – and indeed that was how it felt, a love that burns as bright today as it did all those years ago.

_ Maina Gielgud AO is a British ballet dancer and choreographer whose long career includes dancing with Maurice Béjart, London Festival Ballet and Sadler's Wells. She was artistic director of The Australian Ballet from 1983–96 and The Royal Danish Ballet from 1997–99, and principal coach with the English National Ballet from 2007–12.

NICK CAVE

... we performed it
the best we ever had,
and the best we ever
could, and the best
we ever will.

A single, unforgettable moment at the Sydney Opera House? Two weeks ago, the last night of our Australian tour, standing on the stage, three songs in, trying to explain to the audience the words to the next song, a very personal song, my favourite song of the set, a song called 'Night Raid'.

The Opera House had been refurbished since I last played there, the stage had been rebuilt and was lower now, giving a more direct and evenly balanced sightline with the audience, a more equal gaze. And as I looked into their collective eyes, I became suddenly and disturbingly overwhelmed by this moment of connection, of mutuality – a reciprocal outpouring and intaking of common regard, of need, of love, all these beautiful people – and choking up I turned away, unable to finish my explanation. I think I realised that this would be the last time we would play this song in this format with these extraordinary musicians, Colin and Larry, and the beautiful singers, Wendi, Janet and T Jae, and I had been hit by a kind of grief. Warren, sensing a collapsing on my part, began the song, hitting the first synth chord and then gesturing to the sky, as he is wont to do, and from then on 'Night Raid' just tumbled out, unfolding beautifully, line upon line, one strange image washing away the next, not a soul moving, the song itself hardly breathing, and everyone, all of us in that wonderful hall, the living and the dead, mesmerised by the moment, by the power of the words and the music and, at the end of the song, the band knowing that we performed it the best we ever had, and the best we ever could, and the best we ever will. The audience understanding, too, and Warren looking across at me with knowing eyes, smiling, as he does when, in those rare and spectral moments, we reach beyond the expectations of the song and tug at the hem of the infinite to collude with the divine.

__ Nick Cave is an Australian singer, songwriter, author and ceramic artist, best known as the lead singer of Nick Cave & the Bad Seeds. His body of work ranges from film score composition to sculpture to fiction. Over the last few years his The Red Hand Files website has seen Cave exploring a deeper and more direct relationship with his fans.

Following spread_ Nick Cave brings his Australian Carnage tour with Warren Ellis to an end in the Concert Hall, December 2022. Photo: Ian Laidlaw.

NIKKI GEMMELL

... across the beautiful white birch seats on a messianic wave of adulation and euphoria and affection and, quite possibly, mass insurrection.

Nick Cave in December 2022, as seen from
the Concert Hall audience. Photo: Thea Sholl.

I had never seen anything like this. In the rarefied loveliness of the new concert hall, Nick Cave. Walking/striding/being carried by the people – or is that borne? – across the beautiful white birch seats on a messianic wave of adulation and euphoria and affection and, quite possibly, mass insurrection. (Can he do that? Can we record it? Bugger it and what the heck.)

Cave then stood absolutely still in about, oh, row L perhaps, and sang a rolling extra-long chorus of 'Hand of God' with his feet somehow balanced on the top slender rim of the seats, a tightroper's thickness of a few centimetres at most and with audience members holding him steady, (we've got you, mate, you're one of us, our secret, eh) or at least that's how it felt in this space.

I was front row with my fifteen-year-old, both of us in awe over the entire tender, profane, exhilarating and at times almost unbearably moving concert experience, an early Christmas gift.

Cave entwined his fingers in my girl's several times, once pulled her towards him mesmerically, pulled her close to the hallowed turf of the stage until she broke free reluctantly in confusion and flush, then as he was taking his bows he leant down and threw to her: 'you're gorgeous'; she, of course, was in heaven.

Plus there had been an instructive view throughout the concert (for the muso) of Cave's piano and his preacher's flying fingers and the typed lyric sheets with their handwritten chords on large rectangles of card, her eyes saucers at Warren Ellis playing violin – so relaxed, so cheeky, so chuffed – while lying horizontal on his back on a chair, her eyes wide at percussionist Larry Mullins combining timpani with a drumkit, thrillingly, in a way she'd never seen before; all the possibilities of what music can be, and do. 'Best concert I've ever been to,' she exclaimed at one stage, clutching my arm in ecstasy and I got a little teary at that point, at all the wonder before us, rock and punk and gospel and ballad in one stewy, expletive-filled mix, and at the Opera House of all places; this building that had represented throughout my youth the mother-enforced straitjacket of stuffy ballets and Sunday best and being told not to slump but sit up straight. Yet here, now, this performance space was being cracked open into a raucous, roaring house of profanity and power for the people, all the people.

Cave spoke of his 'yearning' to be back in Australia after too many COVID-years away and yeah, I get that, the corrosiveness of the need in the expat for the hurting blue sky that's in our blood and bones, that will never let us go. And our favourite prodigal son was at home that night, on fire, cracking jokes about degenerate Sydney as only a Victorian can during a fifteen-year-old's baptism of musical fire in a hallowed space. And I was with her all the way, bonded like a parent of a teen can only dream of, but so rarely, fleetingly grasp; as I watched my girl spellbound at the potency of music and the preacher-man performance, at the audience's loving response and at the vast soaring beauty of the space and she wasn't rolling her eyes at me or telling me to get out of her space, but was actually, utterly impressed that I'd dragged her along to this transcendent event, and at the Opera House, for a night neither of us will ever forget.

__ Nikki Gemmell is the author of some twenty-two books, including *Shiver*, *The Bride Stripped Bare*, *The Ripping Tree* and *Dissolve*. Born in Wollongong, she lived in London for many years and has now returned home to Australia.

JORDI SAVALL

Every performance hall has its own character. The Vienna Konzerthaus, the Amsterdam Concertgebouw, the Philharmonie de Paris, the Sydney Opera House: the acoustics of each of these halls have their own specific qualities – and that includes Sydney, which has always been special for the kind of music that we play, early music, historically informed. These qualities are impossible to imitate.

The first impression you have when you arrive is the building itself. The Opera House is spectacular. It's visually incredible. It promises something very special. But for me, the main aspect to consider is what happens inside: the quality of the sound and the way it projects out into the audience. This is the most essential quality.

When the acoustics are good, an instrument or a voice contains certain sounds and colours that become more intense. When they are not, the experience is diminished. How we respond to this environment is up to us as the musicians performing in this hall.

One of the mysteries of music is that it exists only in the moment. This is the case even for a recording, which exists only in your memory once it finishes. You can see the work of a painter in the museum, but you can only hear music from earlier times when it's played. For us, as historically informed musicians, it's like being a living museum. We reproduce sounds and styles as they were at the time of the composer, using the same instruments, the same articulations, the same bowing. And in 2014, when we came to the Opera House with the *Jerusalem* project, we found that our sounds moved freely around the Concert Hall in a very nice way. The renovations came later, too. Other performers might have had different experiences, but for us, the original acoustics of the Concert Hall were very helpful.

For my first recording, back in 1975, we found a nice church outside Paris. It had an airport close by so we were forced to record from 8 pm to 6 am. The French have a lovely phrase for the effort it takes when you're playing, exhausted, at three in the morning: *supplément d'âme*, that extra helping of soul, the supplementary spirit and atmosphere that only really exists in the moment.

In concert, you need to find that *supplément d'âme* every time.
You don't get a second chance. I suspect that this is what we carried
through with us at the Opera House on that April night. It was a complex
program that detailed 2000 years of Jerusalem's history. I remember
listening to the trumpets and the shofars, the ancient instrument
made from a ram's horn, and there was this incredible dissonance
and colour that could be heard all throughout that hall. It was a very
special experience.

    __ Jordi Savall, a Catalan conductor, director, viol player,
       teacher and researcher, is one of the world's most
       influential proponents of early music.

BAZ LUHRMANN

... we put shows on for everybody else, so why don't we put a show on for our friends?

Baz Luhrmann and Catherine Martin tie the knot on the
Opera House set of *La Bohème* in 1997. Photo: Mike Newling.

First, the iconic child's perspective. Growing up in the arts at the National Institute of Dramatic Art and the Sydney Theatre Company – the Sydney Opera House was something we were all very proud of because it symbolised culture in Australia. There'd be unbelievable ordinariness, then all of a sudden BANG – a flash of lightning. The fact that the nation pulled together – whatever the true drama of the building was, whether it was realised the way it should have been or not – the extraordinary commitment that we should have one, and that we should have one that was exceptional, sent a signal to the world that Australia cared about culture. It always struck me that when they did a survey and the question was: 'Do you care about the opera?' the answer was 'No'. But when they asked: 'Do you think we should have an opera house?' the answer was always 'Yes'. I think that's symbolic of the Australian attitude towards the arts. There is a genuine belief in the arts even though we're such a sports culture.

That was my growing-up perspective. Then the really big moment was when Moffatt Oxenbould, then artistic director of The Australian Opera, gave me my little experimental opera company, The Ra Project. Then he did something so radical that it's hard to appreciate now. You might give a young director a Janáček opera, something not very commercial. But Puccini, particularly *La Bohème*, was their money-maker. *La Bohème* keeps the subscribers happy and attracts other walk-ins and tourists. The idea that he was going to hand over *La Bohème* to this rather precocious director in his twenties, who had just done a crazy project with the Sydney Theatre Company, was an outrage.

We cashed in our very small amount of money and, with Catherine Martin and Bill Marron, the designer and associate designer, we went to Italy. I travelled to Torre del Lago, where Puccini wrote the opera, we studied the opera, and the opera houses it was performed in, then we ended up in Paris in an apartment owned by CM's uncle, who had passed, and we designed and created our production of *La Bohème*, which we worked on diligently and profoundly.

Come opening night, on 28 July 1990, Joan Sutherland insisted upon being there. The company didn't really want her to come. They knew she hated modern opera productions and they didn't want her to be negative about it. It's hard to believe now, but at the time the production was considered very, very radical. I believe there were even subscribers cancelling their subscriptions. And Joan was very sceptical about it all.

So, we did the production, and I'll always remember David Hobson, who was playing Rodolfo, weeping in the dark in the end. Then there was a kind of silence, the lights went up, there was a spontaneous standing ovation, and it was led by Joan. Two days later, Fred Blanks, the critic for *The Sydney Morning Herald*, absolutely ripped into it. He ended his review with a reference to the standing ovation and said: 'I sat'. The funny thing was that there were more letters to the *Herald* about our production of *La Bohème* than there were about the crisis building in Iraq and Kuwait. From that moment on, Joan became our greatest supporter.

La Bohème sold out to young people. A new young audience came to opera and it became The Australian Opera's highest-grossing opera. The video version ended up on PBS in America and it played for years. It has had an amazing life. It was a truly romantic thing to do, and it connected us to the Opera House. We became like family members. When you're doing an opera there, there's nothing more thrilling than going in and prepping for the show and everyone going 'toi, toi, toi' and getting to know the whole infrastructure of the Opera House. It's quite beautiful. We revived that production, and we did *A Midsummer Night's Dream* there, too, and that went on to Edinburgh.

When CM and I decided to get married, we thought: we put shows on for everybody else, so why don't we put a show on for our friends? It began with them arriving at a warehouse and these guys came out in Hawaiian shirts, playing violins, a bit *Romeo and Juliet*, and they were all loaded onto buses, not knowing where they were going, and they drove down to the Opera House and were taken in the lift to the stage where we'd built the *L'Amour* sign from *La Bohème* and a kind of church. Then our dear friend Noel Staunton, who worked at the Opera House, floated down from the ceiling dressed as a fairy and married us. Our wedding took place on the stage of what is now called the Joan Sutherland Theatre, and we did it just as a show for our friends and family and it was quite magical.

And it's a magical house. You've really got to put on a good show to compete with the view and the harbour. I love everything about it. It's eccentric, it's romantic, it's strange. It's very Australian.

___ Baz Luhrmann is an Oscar-nominated director, producer and writer known worldwide for his work on film, television, opera and theatre.

Following spread_ A scene from Opera Australia's *La Bohème* in 1993, Opera Theatre. Photo: Kiren Chang. Courtesy of Opera Australia.

La Bohème sold out
to young people.
... It has had an amazing
life. It was a truly
romantic thing to do,
and it connected us
to the Opera House.

WENDY MARTIN

There is a Broadway
tradition of dimming
the marquee lights
outside theatres to
acknowledge the passing
of distinguished artists.
They decided to do
the same for Dad ...

Wendy and Lloyd Martin at the opening of the
Sydney Festival in 2005. Photo: William Yang.

I grew up with the Opera House. The first time I went there, the builders were still on site, and I remember my father showing me John Olsen's mural, *Salute to Slessor's 5 Bells*, shortly after it had been installed. I was there for the opening in 1973. My parents were part of the formal party, among the dignitaries, and, as an eleven-year old, I watched from the Botanic Garden. It was thrilling to be part of it. Before he joined the Opera House, my father, Lloyd Martin, ran the Tivoli circuit; he became managing director at only twenty-four, after his own father died while in America seeking talent. Some of my earliest memories are from being backstage at the Tivoli, watching musicals from the front row of the dress circle on the plush red velvet seats.

I remember the day Dad showed us an advertisement he'd cut out of the paper for a job at the Opera House. And I remember how excited I felt when journalists came to our house to interview him after he was named deputy general manager. The building hadn't opened yet, but it felt like a big deal. It had been his dream to work at the Opera House. Dad took over as general manager in 1978, succeeding Frank Barnes, and remained in the role for nineteen years. In 1997, when he retired, his Opera House season had lasted nearly twenty-five years.

Dad was absolutely committed to his job and never missed an opening night. He was notorious for falling asleep in the theatre, once while sitting between the Duke and Duchess of Kent. That episode even made it into the papers. One night I was with him in the Concert Hall, watching the French jazz violinist Stéphane Grappelli. I was so moved by the performance that I turned to my father and squeezed his hand to acknowledge the wonderful experience we were sharing. His head was leaning back. He was sound asleep.

While the Opera House played a huge role in my early life, I never imagined I would work there myself. But there I was, just before the Sydney Olympics, walking across the Forecourt with a lump in my throat, clutching a job application in my hand. Was it really possible that I could come to work in this extraordinary place every day? When I got the job – I worked as a programmer and producer, later overseeing performance and dance – I always believed it was my responsibility to ensure audiences felt the same sense of magic and wonder inside the theatres as I had felt walking across the Forecourt on that perfect Sydney spring day.

At first, I was reticent to acknowledge I was Lloyd Martin's daughter. Twenty-seven years after it had opened, there were still many staff members, particularly front of house, who had been there from the beginning. I was delighted to discover their fondness for Dad. He loved that I was working at the Opera House. We shared stories of the place and the people and we talked about the business. I always felt his sense of delight when he attended an opening night of a production I had produced or presented.

I left in 2003 and returned two years later. Dad had just found out that his cancer had come back after a decade in remission. He continued going to every Opera House opening night, right to the last months of his life. He died at home, in his bed, on 11 August 2005, just after midnight. From his house in Vaucluse, you could see the Opera House across the harbour. It was always in his eyeline.

Later that day, Opera House management told us how they were going to honour his memory. There is a Broadway tradition of dimming the marquee lights outside theatres to acknowledge the passing of distinguished artists. They decided to do the same for Dad, a man who was very much a person of the theatre.

It was incredibly moving. At dusk that night, when the lights came on across Sydney, we watched the Opera House against the sky. Inside, the shows were on, but the sails outside were bathed in darkness. The building was a shadow, an outline, against the night sky. My brother Simon and I wanted to be up close, so we drove to Bennelong Point, stood on the Forecourt and looked up at the sails. Jørn Utzon had told my father that the sails should only ever be lit as if by the moon. Now it was in shadow. Lloyd was a humble man who would never have imagined such a profoundly beautiful gesture in his honour. We stood there in silence and spoke to him.

___ Wendy Martin began her career as an arts producer for ABC and SBS Television. She went on to become artistic director of the Perth Festival and head of performance and dance at the Southbank Centre, London, and the Sydney Opera House.

LOUIS NOWRA

The play would star Mel Gibson, as the soldier, and Noni Hazlehurst as the woman who hides him.

My uncle, Bob Herbert, and I both had plays on in the Sydney Theatre Company's first year of existence. It was thought that an uncle and nephew had never had plays on in the same season anywhere in Australia before. Richard Wherrett, the artistic director, had chosen my uncle's *No Names... No Pack Drill* for his initial season, as well as mine, *The Precious Woman*. My uncle's was first off the rank, and both plays would be on at the Opera House.

I had only been living in Sydney for a year after shifting from Melbourne. I was associate artistic director of STC, so I had visited the Opera House several times. How to explain my sense of elation every time I approached this magnificent structure? At night it was an enchanting sensory experience; the ferries with their passengers inside like miniature dolls in a light box, the calming waves lapping against the sea wall, the illuminated grin of Luna Park in the distance, the glowing

Noni Hazlehurst and Mel Gibson in Sydney Theatre Company's
No Names … No Pack Drill, directed by George Ogilvie, Drama Theatre,
1980. Photo: Branco Gaica. Courtesy of Sydney Theatre Company.

lights of the bridge as it arched across the harbour, the mirrored moon on the nocturnal water, the briny smell of the sea, the white shells of the Opera House like foamy tongues of waves frozen in time; a modernist and romantic cathedral devoted to art.

My uncle had been a navigator in the Australian Air Force during World War Two and had discovered the power of theatre after seeing Laurence Olivier and Vivien Leigh when they toured Australia after the war. He joined JC Williamson's and began as an electrician, actor, stage manager and director of musicals, but his heart was fixed on becoming a playwright. At fifty-seven, and after decades of trying, he was to have his first professional production of a play. It was set in Kings Cross during the war and was roughly based on my mother harbouring an American soldier who had gone AWOL.

It had taken him many drafts to achieve a tight three-act structure with a strong storyline that could have only been crafted by someone who had closely studied Broadway plays. The play would star Mel Gibson, as the soldier, and Noni Hazlehurst as the woman who hides him. Rehearsals irritated him. We'd have coffee and he'd complain about the director, saying he seemed to be allowing chaos to reign. 'In my days, we'd tell actors where to stand and move on the first day of rehearsal and then fill in the emotions afterwards. He's doing it back to front.' I would calm him down, telling him that it was the modern method of rehearsal. This didn't entirely convince him, but he went along with this strange way of putting on a play.

At the previews, he would alternate between watching the play and the audience's reaction. If he suspected the audience didn't like a line or an action, he would change it. The night before the show opened, he was in despair. 'It's run over by three minutes, two nights in a row. In my day a stage manager would be fired for allowing that.' Again, I had to tell him that this was the contemporary fashion. He nodded unsurely, but said as we parted, 'It's sloppy, that's what it is.'

The opening night came, 15 April 1980, and I agreed to meet him in the foyer. As I approached the Opera House I was in a buoyant mood. I felt so happy for my uncle having a production in such a beautiful building. I knew it was a dream come true for him. But as I entered the foyer, I began to feel nervous for him. The play would seem old fashioned to some, and I hoped this would not tell against him.

The foyer was filling with people I knew. I looked around and spotted my uncle – in fact, I couldn't miss him. He was the only man wearing a tuxedo, looking with his trim moustache and upright bearing like something out of an old Hollywood movie. We greeted each other warmly, though he seemed puzzled. 'Why are these people not dressed up for opening night?' I told him that casual wear was typical for a Sydney show. 'But this is the Opera House. And this is an opening night. In my days even the stage manager wore a tuxedo on opening night.'

I went to the bar to get myself a wine and him an orange juice. The foyer was now packed, and as I made my way back to where he had been standing, I saw him next to the cloak room, holding coats and jackets over his arm. 'What's all this?' I asked. 'Oh,' he said, handing the clothes over to the cloak room attendant, 'they think I'm the cloak room attendant because of my tuxedo.' I felt mortified for him, but he grinned. 'It's fine,' he said, 'I've been going through their pockets.'

We sat together to watch the show. The direction was tight, the acting wonderful and the audience laughed in the right places and at other times were suitably engrossed. The ending produced the required gasp of surprise at the malicious landlady's reveal to the military police that destroys the lovers' lives. It went, as my proud uncle said later, 'like clockwork'. He would return every few nights with a stopwatch to make sure the show didn't go over its allotted time and to tinker with the script if he felt the audience were not reacting how he wanted them to. It was a hit and transferred to the Theatre Royal, making him a small fortune.

For years afterwards he and I laughed about being mistaken for a cloak room attendant and he'd say, 'Well, in the old days, we treated theatre traditions with respect, not like today's scruffy barbarians.'

_ Louis Nowra is an award-winning author, screenwriter and playwright. His most recent book is *Sydney: A Biography*.

FERGUS LINEHAN

After interval, things
started to get looser.

In March 2010, having finished my four years as Sydney Festival director, I was living in London when I received a call one morning from the Sydney Opera House. They asked if I could lend a hand on its Vivid LIVE contemporary music festival, which was to be curated by Lou Reed and Laurie Anderson. I had known Lou through a Sydney Festival co-production with St. Ann's Warehouse, a concert staging of *Berlin*, so I jumped on a plane to New York and dived into an exhilarating, chaotic few months. Lou and Laurie are very particular about their work, but with Vivid they wanted to leave room for spontaneity and the unexpected.

Lou had been particularly interested in a celebration of noise, drone and experimental music, as evidenced by his hugely controversial 1975 release *Metal Machine Music*. In the original liner notes, he wrote: 'Most of you won't like this, and I don't blame you at all.' As well as performing *Metal Machine Music* at Vivid, Lou wanted to gather experimental, industrial bands and sound artists for an evening that he called Noise Night. Many of these artists were accustomed to playing to small but wildly devoted audiences in basements or upstairs bar rooms. To find themselves at the Opera House in a rehearsal room with Lou and Laurie was quite the shock.

But these were all artists who took their work extremely seriously. Their music-making was precise, so there was a need for multiple set-ups, to the point where the stage became a fortress of speaker stacks, cables, routers, keyboards, guitars and risers. Armies of crew were booked as the team tried to get their heads around the endlessly complicated specifications of the show in an impossibly short timeframe.

By mid-afternoon on the day of the concert, 31 May 2010, it became clear we had bitten off far more than we could chew. The 7.30 pm start time arrived with fewer than half the artists having had a chance to sound check. At 8.30 pm, we accepted that time was up and let the audience in. The show started well with a Melbourne band Zond, Japan's Melt-Banana, Boris and local hero Oren Ambarchi showing the depth and diversity in this lesser-known corner of music-making. It was, by any standard, very, very loud.

Following spread_ Lou Reed and Laurie Anderson turning up the volume for Noise Night, in the Concert Hall, part of Vivid LIVE in 2010. Photo: Daniel Boud.

After interval, things started to get looser. The amazing Lucas Abela was showing off his technique of drawing sounds out of a sheet of amplified glass when the glass shattered and flew all over the stage. The crew tried desperately to clear away the glass and mop up the blood while those of us backstage began to accept that we had lost control of the running order.

By the time Lou and Laurie came on stage for a sort of all-star finale, it was extremely late and much of the audience had run for final buses and ferries. Pretty much anyone could walk on, pick up an instrument and start playing. Stage management had no idea who was playing, who was backstage, or how and when this wall of sound would ever end. Out front, the crew was frantically trying to figure out what or who they were mixing, and only the most committed audience members had remained in their seats. The front of house staff wondered if they were ever going to get home. Soon, I too was walking around on the stage, in front of Lou, waving at him to get off. He ignored me and played on until almost everyone had left. Eventually, we just turned the house lights on and the final fifty or sixty people shuffled to the exits and staggered off home with their ears ringing.

It's easy to portray a night like this as a funny story of rock'n'roll excess but, looking back, it feels like we were party to something important. The fact the Opera House was willing and able to embrace the improvised chaos of this concert was important to many of us who were there that night. For a moment, the meticulous planning that characterises most Opera House performances had been forgotten, and we had to lean back into 'seat of your pants' reactions that we hadn't used since our days running small theatre companies or touring penniless bands.

The New Yorker's Alex Ross once spoke of how classical music lived under the cloud of 'a terrible fear of being seen as vulgar or careless'. It would be easy to see how this might also be the case in a venue as prestigious as the Sydney Opera House. Noise Night reminded us that even though the Opera House team are consummate professionals, they are also capable of handling extremes of spontaneity and intuition.

Lou Reed could have lived out his days picking up multi-million-dollar fees to perform past hits in massive arenas. Instead, he remained committed to the uncomfortable search for ideas that might move things forward. For many of us at the time, Noise Night felt more like a prison riot than a concert, but in retrospect it was an emboldening reminder that, as Nietzsche wrote, 'One must still have chaos in one, to give birth to a dancing star.'

__ Fergus Linehan was artistic director of the Dublin Theatre Festival, Sydney Festival, Vivid LIVE at the Sydney Opera House and the Edinburgh International Festival. He is a Fellow of the Royal Society of Edinburgh and co-chair of IMPACT Scotland, the organisation charged with building Edinburgh's new concert hall. He lives in Sydney and in 2023 was named CEO of Carriageworks.

Soon, I too was walking around on the stage, in front of Lou, waving at him to get off. He ignored me and played on until almost everyone had left.

BILL HENSON

In September 1985, I had been in Sydney installing an exhibition at Garry Anderson's gallery in Darlinghurst that was due to open the following evening. To clear my head after what had been a long day of up and down ladders, fine-tuning the various groupings from my *Untitled 1983–84* series, I decided to walk back into the city where I was staying. It was one of those balmy Sydney evenings.

I'd been preoccupied with this imagery of baroque architecture and just how I might balance it with the images of faces and figures that formed the other component of the series. On my way back, I found myself near the Opera House and took a detour up into the building for what was, back then, my first visit. My mind had been full of images of architecture all day and this firsthand experience of the internal spaces of the Opera House remains the most powerful memory of that night and, particularly, of being struck by ascending the southern staircase under a low ceiling and suddenly feeling the roof evaporate into a vast lofty cavern overhead.

Image LAT-99 from *Untitled 1983–84* by Bill Henson.   175

There was this unfolding sense of volume, an architectural device used over the millennia and something I'd seen when visiting Chartres and some of the great Cistercian monasteries, and it was accompanied by an apprehension of entering into some kind of profound dialogue of significance. I was surprised to discover that this had found its echo – against the odds – in a modern building.

In my experience of working in sacred structures while photographing them, whether the temples of ancient Egypt, or perhaps the northern European churches with their soaring fan-vaulted arches – inspired, as they were, by the interlocking branches of the great and ancient forests – I often experienced a gathering sense of mystery. More recently, in a curious reversal of these expanding spaces, I feel on entering the vast lobbies and foyers of modern corporate architecture that everything after the initial impression becomes smaller, not bigger – cramped elevators, low ceilinged offices and narrow corridors. Perhaps, as Kenneth Clark once observed, this has come about because my historical examples were built to the glory of God whereas the more recent ones were built to the glory of Mammon.

Our present subject represents one of the rare examples of a contemporary building that set out to be a symbol for the sacredness of something other than money. Art.

Ascending that web of staircases as they climb up through the gigantic arching beams of the structure, I'm always reminded of a cardinal quality of great art, including architecture, despite its ergonomic imperative to serve a functional purpose. And that is that not everything is revealed at once, nor can it even be taken in, really, from one vantage point.

That we could, in commissioning this building, have briefly experienced a public state-of-mind that approached the Cistercians' 'building as a form of worship' now seems remarkable. Imagine the attitude to life that accompanied those who began the construction of Chartres in the knowledge that neither they, nor even their great grandchildren, would live to see it completed.

The Opera House stands as an example of that against-the-odds-ness that the American poet and critic Peter Schjeldahl described thus: 'Beauty makes a case for the sacredness of something – winning the case suddenly and irrationally.'

... a contemporary building that set out to be a symbol for the sacredness of something other than money. Art.

__ Bill Henson is one of Australia's most distinguished artists. His darkly enigmatic photographs have been exhibited extensively both in Australia and around the world over a period of more than four decades.

ELENA KATS-CHERNIN

During rehearsals I had gone into the orchestra pit to look around, which is something I still do. I enjoy seeing how the pit works. It's like exploring inside a body. Every part has to be healthy and in good condition.

Alexa Heckmann in *Wild Swans*, 2003. Photo: Branco Gaica. Courtesy of The Australian Ballet.
Following spread_ Alexa Heckmann in The Australian Ballet's *Wild Swans*, 2003. Photo: Branco
Gaica. Courtesy The Australian Ballet. Lighting design by Stephen Wickham, choreography by
Meryl Tankard, costume design by Angus Strathie and set design by Régis Lansac.

In 1975, when I arrived in Australia from Moscow, I could read music but spoke only basic English. I started studying at the Conservatorium of Music almost straight away. It wasn't until later that year, though, when I was invited by some of the girls in my class to join a choir, that I first visited the Sydney Opera House.

It was December. They said we were going to be singing Christmas carols, but I didn't know what they were talking about. We didn't have carols in Russia. I went along to rehearsals anyway and then, before I knew it, I found myself on stage at the Opera House, wearing some kind of a cloak. (We were supposed to be angels.)

I just saw all this as part of my social life. I wish I had understood the magnitude of the moment.

Many years later, I wrote a piece called 'Deep Sea Dreaming', which Meryl Tankard was putting together for the opening ceremony of the Sydney Olympics, the part when Nikki Webster went up into the sky. I went along to the Opera House to see Simone Young record the piece with the Sydney Symphony Orchestra and Sydney Children's Choir. It was my first time working with Simone, and I still remember sitting there alone in the audience as they played. A little person in this big hall and this amazing group of people recording a piece of mine that was going to be heard by millions around the world. I definitely felt a sense of occasion that time, like a shiver. I felt very honoured.

The most emotional moment for me came in 2003, inside the Joan Sutherland Theatre. I was working on *Wild Swans*, another Meryl Tankard ballet. During rehearsals I had gone into the orchestra pit to look around, which is something I still do. I enjoy seeing how the pit works. It's like exploring inside a body. Every part has to be healthy and in good condition.

On opening night, 2 May 2003, the belly opened and I heard the first notes being played for an audience, and it was amazing. For the rest of that performance, it was a collective experience for me, trying to feel what other people were feeling. You want a reaction. You don't want them to think it's bland or boring. You want them to feel something.

At the end, I went up on stage with the whole team to take a bow, and the applause was rapturous. I really wanted to savour that moment. I still have the pink skirt I was wearing when I took that bow. (Later on, the 'Eliza Aria' from that ballet became famous in England because it was used as a jingle for a bank commercial. And in Australia, Phillip Adams used it on his *Late Night Live* show on Radio National.)

Wild Swans was my first big ballet, a ninety-minute production, and I'd given it my heart and my soul. So, the bow that night – saying thank you to the audience, to the orchestra, to everyone – felt very precious. I went to every performance after that night, too. It was fun to be a fly on the wall, listening to people at interval, because no one knew who I was, and I couldn't stay away.

The Opera House is a special building. Just walking through the stage door feels like a privilege. It feels like that every time. Back when I was living in Russia, it was always this incredible, mysterious building, and of course I never dreamed I would be able to walk inside it, let alone to work there.

That's why I never take anything for granted. Every morning, I'm grateful that I have another day. Another day to walk over to my piano and another day to write more music.

__ Elena Kats-Chernin AO is one of Australia's leading composers, having created works for theatre, ballet, symphony orchestras and chamber ensembles as well as scores for silent films. Born in Tashkent, Uzbekistan, she trained in Moscow followed by Sydney after immigrating to Australia and, lastly, thanks to a German exchange scholarship, in Hanover where she lived and worked before returning in 1994 to Sydney. She has won many awards since then, including the Australian Women in Music Awards in 2022 for Artistic Excellence.

TIM SHARP

__ Based in Brisbane, Tim Sharp is an Australian artist with autism and creator of Laser Beak Man. His colourful, happy art was made into an animated TV series and a theatre production that included a 2020 season at the Sydney Opera House. Tim's work has been sold to collectors around the world.

Tim Sharp, and his mother Judy, in conversation in the Utzon Room with Jac
Marriott for World Autism Awareness Day in April 2019. Photo: Jacquie Manning.
Following spread_ In 2014, Tim Sharp shared his story on the Concert Hall
stage as part of TEDxSydney. Here he recalls the significance of that moment.

GRAEME MURPHY

That first performance was such a turning point. We loved the Opera House because we could take risks there as artists. It was a privilege not to have to toe any particular line.

Janet Vernon AM in *Some Rooms (The Bathroom)*, the Graeme Murphy production
that transformed the fortunes of the Sydney Dance Company. Drama Theatre,
1983. Photo: Branco Gaica. Courtesy of Sydney Dance Company.

This story begins in 1977 with a triple bill at the Sydney Opera House that was both terrifying and wonderful. Our first full-length production, *Poppy*, followed in 1978, at the Theatre Royal, and that set off a roll of work. Our audience was building and we were feeling good. The profile of the Sydney Dance Company was rising. We were gung-ho. We were confident.

In 1983, we were planning a new show called *Some Rooms*. There was a lot of buzz: we had gorgeous music, a great concept and we had Paul Mercurio, the rising star, in the cast. The costumes were being made and everything was ready, but then we learned that we had to embark on an extended regional tour as a condition of our funding. The end of that tour left us with huge holes in the coffers. As a result, a man moved into our studios, took over our finances and told us to start selling anything of value.

Around that time, someone rang up Frank Barnes, then general manager of the Opera House and a great champion of our work. I don't know what was said, but he called us to say the Opera House was going to bankroll the season of *Some Rooms*. That was extraordinary news. It was only a few days before opening night in November. Until that moment, we thought we were preparing for our final season because it was never going to be enough to pay back our debts. Frank's decision changed our world and led to a 31-year relationship between the Opera House and the Sydney Dance Company.

The show went gangbusters. It exceeded our expectations to the extent that we were confident enough at the end to kiss the liquidator goodbye. Out of that production came a touring schedule that took us around Australia and overseas, including Paris, New York and London. We toured it everywhere. It was a pivotal moment and I'll never ever stop being grateful.

Some Rooms was in the repertoire all the way up to 2004. It was controversial, but it was entertaining, too. In 1989, when I took a sabbatical, my wife Janet Vernon ran the company and she toured it to America. David Bowie knocked on the door of her dressing room after one performance. He'd been in the audience and wanted to have a chat. Before he left, he stubbed his cigarette out in the sink and Janet was appalled. I was more appalled that she didn't keep it.

That first performance was such a turning point. We loved the Opera House because we could take risks there as artists. It was a privilege not to have to toe any particular line. If you were watching, you could be astonished, appalled, disgusted or delighted at any given time.

The most precious compliment I ever get is when someone comes up to me, thirty or forty years later, and tells me they were there and that they remember this part or that part. Those things become more important than a recorded version. I selfishly delight in the idea that no one can own or possess these works. They can share it. They can recall it. They can forget it. But they don't ever own it. That's what's so weird and wonderful about dance.

__ Graeme Murphy AO is a dancer, choreographer and director. He danced with The Australian Ballet, Sadler's Wells Ballet and Ballets Félix Blaska before taking over as artistic director of the Sydney Dance Company, a role he held for thirty-one years, during which he created more than fifty works, including thirty full-length productions.

MARCIA HINES

To hear those enormous voices coming from the choir in the Opera House: Wow, just wow. The songs sounded better than I remembered.

Marcia Hines sings in a New Year's Eve Concert at
the Opera House in 1985. Photo: Don McMurdo.
Following spread_ Marcia Hines in *Velvet Rewired*
in the Studio in 2022. Photo: Daniel Boud.

Any performer worth their salt feels nervous before a performance. Terribly nervous, though I can only really speak for myself on this point. That nervous feeling helps to keep me on my toes. When I walk out on stage, any stage, I always want to do my best. I want it to be a memorable performance, every time, and those nerves keep me in check. You need to gauge the situation correctly, though, so they don't take you over.

Nerves come down on you anywhere, but the anticipation is even more enhanced when you're getting ready for one of the stages at the Sydney Opera House. The biggest one especially: there's nothing like the Concert Hall. It has a presence. I felt it on my first experience, more than three decades ago, and it's a sensation that has returned to me every time in all the shows in all the years that have passed since then, whether I'm playing my own songs in the Concert Hall, singing with others on the Forecourt or, more recently, when I stepped out as the Diva for *Velvet Rewired*, downstairs in the Studio. When we took *Australian Idol* to the Opera House – I was a judge for seven consecutive years – we'd sit in the booth and watch all the kids perform and then the winner would be announced against that incredible backdrop. It's one of the most famous buildings in the world. And those stages, they're nothing to sneeze at.

That first performance of mine was a gospel show. It was a Friday, 12 April 1985, the first of two shows. I was singing church songs, Black American spirituals, with the Sydney Philharmonia Choirs and an amazing pianist called Julian Lee. That first night, when I stepped out to sing, was one of those moments I'll keep in my mind forever. The sound was outstanding. The voices of the choir and the acoustics in that room were like nothing I'd ever heard before.

Australian audiences knew some part of what I could do. I was a recording artist. I had recorded a couple of albums that had done well. So people knew the pop songs, but they didn't know this other side of me, and this was an important part of who I was. It was like going back to my roots. Most Black kids are brought up in church in America and those songs were a big part of my upbringing. I used to travel with my aunt every Sunday to churches around Boston, listening closely as she led the choir, singing those glorious gospel sounds.

The show was called *Spirituals: Music of the Heart & the Soul*. As well as *The Lord's Prayer*, from David Fanshawe's 1972 *African Sanctus*, the program featured material like 'Oh Happy Day', 'He's Got the Whole World in His Hands' and 'Rock My Soul'. To hear those enormous voices coming from the choir in the Opera House: Wow, just wow. The songs sounded better than I remembered. The beauty of the voices, as well as the arrangements that had been put together by the pianist and Peter Seymour, the musical director, took the experience to another level.

That night, the Opera House just felt right, but it's always been like that for me. That sense of awe never really fades. These days, whenever I drive towards the building, the excitement is palpable. Some people only stare at the outside of that incredible building, never having had the pleasure of going inside. I don't like to blow my own trumpet, but I'm blessed to have been a small part of the Opera House story. I'm blessed, too, to still have a gig there and to still be relatively relevant after all this time. These are stories I'll be telling my grandkids, content in the knowledge that the Opera House will still be there long after I'm gone.

— Marcia Hines has released twenty-two albums in a career spanning five decades. She moved from Boston to Sydney at sixteen to star in the Australian production of *Hair*, appearing in a variety of productions in the coming years, from *Jesus Christ Superstar* to *Australian Idol*, where she was a judge. She was inducted into the ARIA Hall of Fame in 2007 and received an Order of Australia (AM) in 2009 for her services to the Australian entertainment industry as a performer, judge and mentor, and to the community through a range of charitable organisations.

RICHARD TOGNETTI

From pot to table, it was six weeks. The pot was in Western Australia, up at the Ningaloo Reef. We started filming, creating music, thinking how it would all tie together, then on 23 July 2012, at the end of a national tour that had begun in Darwin earlier that month, we walked onto the Concert Hall stage and played this film for a Sydney Opera House audience. It was unique, bespoke. No one had ever done anything like it before or since. And the audience was amazing.

The Opera House could only dream of those kinds of crowds. For a start, it was packed with surfers, classical music people, audiences who come for the Australian Chamber Orchestra without really knowing that much about what we were doing, and people who had come for the visual experience. With filmed footage by Jon Frank and Mick Sowry, we played music by Bach, Alice in Chains, Shostakovich, Stephen Pigram, Iain Grandage and Ligeti. We finished with the Cavatina from Beethoven's String Quartet in B flat major, Opus 130 – and that was when I realised that the iceberg had floated away. The classical music world was the iceberg and the iceberg was melting. No longer did we belong to the academy, to the classical music world. It was a splintering-off moment and it was happening in the Opera House.

Every major classical music venue around the world is going through this transformation. If they're not, they're going to atrophy. To not be aware of the temperature of the water as a frog is a dangerous thing.

I wasn't thinking those things during the performance. When you're performing, you're head down. You're not performing well unless you're in a kind of Zen space. But I realised straight afterwards the importance of it. I think a lot of people did.

The actual music, the notes, are separate from how they're perceived. We all perceive them differently, but the time has come for a massive reappraisal in how they're received by the general public and the academy. *The Reef* was part of that reappraisal. Certain people and institutions were aghast, but that was a defining moment because it was when our finger went up at the academy, the gatekeepers.

We were building a portal through which people who didn't know what classical music was about could access that music. I'm not talking about dressing it up in silly clothes or cheapening the notes. The integrity was there; it was underlined. But in this film, and that performance, people were having a Stendhal experience with a Beethoven Cavatina. And instead of being celebrated for that, the response from certain people was a two-finger cross. That's when we knew we were doing something right and revelatory.

As I wrote in the program, *The Reef* was about creating a sonic dialogue with the mysterious wonder that is surfing: 'Within all of us is the capacity for wonder. In some, it just lies dormant.'

__ As artistic director and lead violin of the Australian Chamber Orchestra, Richard Tognetti AO has received honorary doctorates from three Australian universities and was made a National Living Treasure in 1999. In 2017 he was awarded the JC Williamson Award for longstanding service to the live performance industry.

Following spread_ Satu Vänskä and the Australian Chamber Orchestra during a performance of *The Reef* in the Concert Hall, July 2012. Photo: Prudence Upton. Courtesy of the Australian Chamber Orchestra.

NGAIIRE

My first show at the Sydney Opera House, on 10 November 2022, was a career highlight. I'd seen other artists there, of course, and dreamed of doing it myself, but never really felt I would reach the calibre of those who perform somewhere so prestigious. And to do it with the Sydney Symphony Orchestra, as I did that night, and on the Forecourt no less, was just huge. Clearly this was not going to be just another gig.

After sound check, I had an hour to get ready. I was busy making sure my family could get in and finishing off other details. Other people were running around making sure everything was going smoothly. There was so much happening. And I was nervous. I rarely get nervous before shows, but everything that night felt more heightened than usual. I wanted to be especially present.

We were in a trailer behind the Forecourt stage, waiting to go on, and that's when we decided to play Crowded House. It was just a spur of the moment thing. It was me and the backing vocalists and the idea came to us. What were we going to play to vibe things up?

The farewell Crowded House concert, on the same stage in 1996, still feels so iconic. Most of us were kids then but it was such an important moment, which is probably why we thought of it that night. The music played through a Bluetooth speaker as we tried to capture some of that Crowded House energy for ourselves. We sang along to a few hits: 'Better Be Home Soon', 'Distant Sun', 'Don't Dream It's Over'. It was really hot outside, a bunch of flowers had been delivered from someone at the Opera House, and all of us were gathered around the air conditioning unit, singing along to the music of Crowded House. It was the calm before the storm. One of the only still moments I had leading up to the show.

Then we walked out to a sea of people. The orchestra started and I was carried through a show that felt like it finished in a second. At one point, I closed my eyes to sing 'Fall into My Arms', a song I wanted to deliver as honestly and truthfully as I could, and when I opened my eyes, it looked like everyone in the crowd had their phone lights out. That's never happened to me before in concert. I was quite shocked, it was beautiful.

On that stage, standing there, looking at the Opera House and the Harbour Bridge and the city and all these people: it's the kind of scene that commands a different kind of performance. Any skills or professionalism you've learned over your career come to the fore in a situation like that.

I was enjoying every single moment, hyperaware of what was going on around me, even though it was over too quickly. We usually end on 'Fall into My Arms', but this time we ended on 'Glitter' because we wanted to leave people on a high. Then we took a moment to receive the applause. I used to scurry away after shows, but Paul Mac gave me the great advice to stand and take the applause. So that's what we did. We stood there on the Forecourt and received the applause. After that, everything was a blur. All I wanted to do was to steal away somewhere quiet and reflect on what had just happened.

_ Since coming to national attention as a contestant on *Australian Idol*, Papua New Guinea-born Ngaiire, or Ngaire Laun Joseph, has defied genre and expectations. Her fusion of electronic neo-soul, gospel and R&B pop – filtered through her experiences as a First Nations woman – has seen her garner multiple award nominations and perform alongside the likes of Sufjan Stevens, Alicia Keys and Flume.

Above_ Crowded House on the Forecourt in 1996. Photo: Tony Mott.
Following spread_ Ngaiire performing with the Sydney Symphony
Orchestra on the Forecourt in 2022. Photo: Prudence Upton.

WENDY BLACKLOCK

The challenge ahead
of us, as producers,
was obvious. If my
job was to present
Australian stories, why
weren't we hearing
from the people who
lived here first?

Jack Davis in *The Dreamers*, 1983.
Courtesy of Mitchell Library, State Library
of NSW, MLMSS 10315/Box 2X.

What counts as innovative? Robert Hughes talked about the 'shock of the new', but the new doesn't stay new for long. It doesn't even stay shocking. For most of the 1980s, when I worked to nurture a generation of new talent on the Australian stage, the scope of this challenge was clear.

In 1975, the Commonwealth Government established the Australia Council to raise the standard of the arts, to encourage more Australians to become involved and to promote cultural heritage. I was a performer at the time, having worked in the UK, New Zealand and across Australia, but I joined The Australian Elizabethan Theatre Trust because I wanted to become a producer. In 1982, the Australia Council announced that part of its annual grant to the Trust should be spent on theatre development, innovative theatre especially. In response, the Australian Content Department was created, and I was made general manager.

One day, an old friend, Brian Syron, walked into my office with an idea of what was to become our first Aboriginal and Torres Strait Islander production: a remount of Robert Merritt's play, *The Cake Man*. The production was invited to the World Theatre Festival in Colorado, setting off overseas after three previews at the Parade Theatre in Kensington, later returning for a season in Brisbane and Melbourne.

Encouraged by this success, we went in search of more First Nations voices. The shows coming out of Western Australia were particularly interesting. Word reached us about an exciting new work by Noongar writer Jack Davis. We dispatched a Trust representative to Perth, and the result was a seventeen-week national tour for *The Dreamers*. It boasted an impressive team: choreography by Ernie Dingo, direction by Andrew Ross, music by Ted Wilks and Richard Walley, plus a cast that included Davis, Dingo and lots of family members.

The Dreamers was the first Aboriginal and Torres Strait Islander play to tour Australia. While First Nations performers had starred in a 1974 production of Michael Boddy's *The Cradle of Hercules*, this was believed to be the first Aboriginal and Torres Strait Islander play presented at the Opera House. It was co-produced by the Ensemble Theatre, the National Theatre Company of Western Australia and The Australian Elizabethan Theatre Trust. As Harry Kippax wrote in *The Sydney Morning Herald* on 6 October 1983: 'This admirable production offers a rare, enriching theatrical experience.'

I remember sitting in the audience one afternoon at the Playhouse, watching a matinee performance with school children. At that time, older white Australians like myself had a limited connection with Aboriginal and Torres Strait Islander peoples and their stories. Suddenly I found myself among a young audience responding enthusiastically to the story in front of them. They laughed at the jokes, and they understood the family problems that Davis depicted, even though the specific experience may have been a long way from their own lives. It was the most extraordinary sense of connection, an engagement that came without any of the baggage that made some of the older audiences hesitant. I have put a lot of shows into the Opera House over the years, but that matinee was particularly special because of the way it broadened the perspectives of those in the audience, myself included.

It also opened doors for Jack Davis. After this production, I commissioned him to write *No Sugar*, the first part of a trilogy that included *The Dreamers* and that would conclude with *Barungin*. *No Sugar* was invited to represent Australia at the World Theatre Festival in Vancouver, Canada, in 1986, and also toured the UK in 1989.

The challenge ahead of us, as producers, was obvious. If my job was to present Australian stories, why weren't we hearing from the people who lived here first? These days there are more opportunities for Aboriginal and Torres Strait Islander writers and artists, but back then it was more difficult to find the necessary levels of support. As we could see, though, the time was right. Audiences were open and were ready to hear these stories.

— Wendy Blacklock AM is a performer and producer whose work has supported a wide range of Australian cultural activity across three decades. After a successful career on stage, radio and TV, she went on to become general manager of the Australian Content Department of The Australian Elizabethan Theatre Trust and later led Performing Lines, a not-for-profit company that champions independent arts and First Nations work as well as promotes Australian culture to audiences abroad.

WESLEY ENOCH

The Sydney Opera House Drama Theatre on 18 January 2014. It's
the opening night of *Black Diggers* and there is an amazing array of
dignitaries in the audience: state governors, the head of the Australian
Army, government ministers, the Belgian Ambassador, Elders who have
travelled from around the country and so many more. The introductions
at the preshow function seemed as long as the speeches themselves,
as name after name and their official titles were read out.

      Black Diggers was a play chronicling the participation of
Indigenous Australians in World War One. The world was on the brink of the
100th anniversary commemorations of the Great War and this production
had been commissioned by Sydney Festival and the Queensland Theatre
Company. After years of research, including a trip to Flanders Fields to
visit the war graves of Aboriginal soldiers, this was the world premiere
and I kept looking for a sign from the Elders that everything was okay.

      Telling Elders that the story of their great uncle or grandfather
who had fought and died in World War One was going to be told on stage
at the Opera House … well, it gave them a sense of being seen, their
untold family story being elevated for the world to hear. They puffed up
with pride that the Opera House would host their story – a story their
family had always known – that their family member had always fought
for Country, always protected it.

But we hadn't seen the lights and sound, costume and sets until we got into the theatre and opening night was just four days later. We didn't know if it was any good, or whether we had adequately served the memories of these long-gone Black soldiers and their families. The normal nervousness was compounded by the expectations of all those who had gathered to witness this truth-telling. I nervously looked down the row of seats to see what the Elders were thinking. Their faces were motionless.

The Opera House demands the attention of the country. It's one of the truly international Australian icons, but people sometimes forget it is a complex of working theatres. It is also a crucible for important ideas and the site of many significant First Nations stories, from Bennelong to Bangarra to *Black Diggers*.

So when, at the end of the show, the audience leapt to their feet, cheering and clapping loudly, it felt like something had started, something that could not be taken back. I looked down the row and saw tears rolling down cheeks, faces animated with wonder and pride. *Black Diggers* went on to tour the whole country to sell-out crowds, but I know there was some magic from that night that travelled with it.

__ Wesley Enoch AM, a Quandamooka man from Minjerribah (Stradbroke Island), is a playwright and director whose work has received multiple honours over the years. His creative leadership includes resident director of the Sydney Theatre Company, Ilbijerri Aboriginal Torres Strait Islander Theatre Cooperative, associate artistic director at Belvoir St Theatre, artistic director of the Sydney Festival and artistic director of the Queensland Theatre Company.

Following spread_ A scene from *Black Diggers*, January 2014.
Photo: Jamie Williams. Courtesy of Sydney Festival.

JOHN OLSEN

When I went to see Kenneth Slessor, he was working as a journalist, his poetical self long since disappeared, and he told me a story. It was the story of an artist who drowned in Sydney opposite the place where the Opera House now stands.

The story went like this. It was a Saturday night. There was much jollity. They heard there was a party that night in Mosman, so they all went down to the ferry. Joe Lynch, the cartoonist, was with them. It had been a rainy day and Joe had two bottles of beer in each pocket of his overcoat. And so they all got on to the ferry and then, when they were near what is now the Opera House, a big liner passed by, the ferry jostled in the turbulence, and after a while someone said: 'Where's Joe?'

Joe had fallen overboard, anchored down by those bottles of beer. A true Australian death.

My mural was commissioned by the Sir William Dobell Art Foundation in 1971, two years before the building opened, and the same year that Slessor died. It was appropriate, I thought, that it would be based on Slessor's 'Five Bells'. Particularly because it emphasises the time factor, and the time factor really hung over the Opera House throughout its long construction. At one point, there had even been talk that they should abandon the project altogether. It was put about in the media that it would be better to put the money into hospitals and education. The usual thing.

The opening lines of Slessor's poem are now famous:

Time that is moved by little fidget wheels
Is not my Time, the flood that does not flow.
Between the double and the single bell
Of a ship's hour, between a round of bells
From the dark warship riding there below,
I have lived many lives, and this one life
Of Joe, long dead, who lives between five bells.

We carried the unfinished mural up to the site in five sections then we worked to finish it onsite. It had taken two years but had to be finished in the Opera House itself. People liked it, but there was a team of workers laying the purple carpet and one of them said his five-year-old could do better than that. I told them to go and see Rudy Komon, the art dealer.

It was a magnificent spot, facing the harbour. This is what I wrote in my journal when we visited the northern foyer in February 1972: 'I like its inside outside feeling ... The way it optically sweeps to Circular Quay on one side, sky above and then (it) rhythmically swings down towards the heads.'

Not only was 'Five Bells' a wonderful poem, and one that happens to have parallels with the Opera House, but it also has a sense of place. That blue luminescence in the mural is the equivalent of water on the harbour, the phosphorescence. It's supposed to be seen at night. The feeling of flying over Sydney Harbour but also sinking beneath the sea. Between the poem and the site, there's a fusion that makes me very happy. It's fresh. It's elegiac. And it's got these rich moods of the harbour in it.

But I remember the day I got in touch with Jørn Utzon, who by that time had gone back to Denmark. I had met him only once, but I wanted his views on what I was doing. Looking at the site, he said, you should make it move east to west so it merges visually with the harbour. He liked the concept. To get his affirmation in that call was a great help to me. He could see it was very important.

Incidentally, Joe's body was never found.

___ John Olsen AO, who died in April 2023, was one of
Australia's most celebrated artists. Born in Newcastle,
he lived in England, Spain and Portugal, later returning to
Australia, where landscapes became a dominant passion
in his work. His awards include the Archibald, Wynne
and Sulman prizes, and he is represented in all major
galleries across the country.

Following spread_ John Olsen with his mural *Salute to Slessor's 5 Bells*
in the Concert Hall Northern Foyer, 2015. Photo: Daniel Boud.

LINDY HUME

It's one of the things
I still love about opera,
that when you're up
close to a singer you
can actually feel it
physically.

Margreta Elkins as Adalgisa in Opera Australia's *Norma*, Opera Theatre,
1978. Photo: William Moseley. Courtesy of Opera Australia

There was a sense of fate when I first walked into that building. When I turned up to the Opera House that day, I was a dancer, and only sixteen. Somebody told me I could pick up work as a supernumerary in the opera. I didn't know what that meant but went along anyway.

The production was Bellini's *Norma* and the director was Sandro Sequi, not that I knew anything about those names at the time. I signed in and walked upstairs. Then came the awe of passing through the Green Room and going to the rehearsal room and being moved around with all the other members of the cast. Suddenly *she* walked in and the whole room's focus shifted to her. She started to sing and I thought: 'I know who you are.' That was the first opera I ever heard live, Joan Sutherland singing 'Casta Diva' a metre away from me.

I felt like I was swimming in the whole experience. What on earth was going on? The singers, the chorus, everything surrounding me: it was the ultimate immersion in the whole madness and glory and wonder of it all. Richard Bonynge was quite sharp with her during the rehearsal. I thought to myself that he was being incredibly rude to that grand lady. I later realised he was married to that grand lady.

I don't know whether my life would be the same had I not been dragged into that rehearsal. It was such an extraordinary phenomenon. It's one of the things I still love about opera, that when you're up close to a singer you can actually feel it physically. And to have someone like her singing that particular aria – especially when you've heard neither the aria nor her – I remember being pretty overwhelmed. She was a substantial physical presence. Everything about the occasion was intriguing. The mark-ups on the floor, the fact the choirs seemed to know what they were doing, the fact that everyone was singing in Italian. It was like another planet.

That was the beginning of my time in opera: *Norma* opened on 5 July 1978. I had listened to opera but I don't think I had ever been to one, and I certainly hadn't imagined it would be something I would be involved in. But through that experience, and my subsequent years as a dancer with the company, I became completely infatuated.

Twelve years later, I ended up directing Dame Joan's final performance at the Opera House. It was a revival of a terribly old-fashioned production of *Les Huguenots*, complete with wobbly scenery, painted clothes and false perspectives – but that didn't matter because everyone was there for her.

I also remember the physical experience of the building, how it imprinted itself onto the psyche: those big windows in the middle of the Green Room, the dressing rooms with their views of the harbour. It was an extraordinary space. I was a dancer, and I knew nothing other than dance, so being there that day seemed like being connected to something huge. It was an introduction into a bigger world.

— Lindy Hume AM is one of Australia's leading directors, acknowledged internationally for fresh interpretations of a wide variety of repertoire, and for progressive artistic leadership of several Australian arts organisations, including Opera Queensland (2012–17), Sydney Festival (2010–12) and Perth International Arts Festival (2004–07). She was also the first artistic director of West Australian Opera (1992–96), artistic director of Victoria State Opera and then OzOpera (1996–2001).

BARRIE KOSKY

Three postcards stick out in my mind. The first was in October 1990. Joan Sutherland's farewell performance at the Sydney Opera House. She was doing *Les Huguenots*, that long, large, historical Meyerbeer opera, and the snapshot I have is of Joan Sutherland, in her huge 16th century costume, leaning against the billiard table in the Green Room, eating a bag of chips with the technicians while they played. I've never been able to listen to Joan Sutherland again without thinking of that moment, which was pretty fabulous.

The second postcard comes from 12 August 1995, when I had just received one of the worst responses to an opera production in the history of the Opera House: I was booed on the opening night of Verdi's *Nabucco*. It's very rare for Australian audiences to boo like that. I'm used to it now; I've had thirty-five years of it. But it was new then, and it was something of a badge of honour that I had made a certain section – and it was a section, a lot of the audience loved it – decide to take their revenge in that particular Australian way. (It wasn't like German booing, which is full throttle.) It was a historic night at the Opera House because it had never happened like that before. Ever. I was terrified and elated and I was in the lift going to the dressing rooms after the show when the Whitlams, Gough and Margaret, appeared in front of me. You can imagine: the doors opened and it's Gough and Margaret. I didn't know them at all, and Margaret turned around to me, and I thought, 'Oh God, here we go.' And she just went: 'Bravo, maestro.' And then Gough said: 'I absolutely loved it.' And then proceeded for two minutes as the lift was moving to give me their potted version. So, Margaret Whitlam's deep, basso profundo 'bravo maestro' is what I remember about the night rather than Sydney's middle-class audience not liking what they saw on stage.

The third postcard was two years later. I did a production of *Tartuffe* for the Sydney Theatre Company, which had a great cast including David Wenham and Mitchell Butel. From opening night on 15 May 1997, it was critically savaged by one of the biggest audiences the STC had ever had at the Opera House. We reinvented Molière's story to a contemporary

Australian Christmas, a hot summer Christmas. There was a particularly wild set by Peter Corrigan, there was lip syncing, 'Daisy' Wenham did a huge dance with a turkey, and there was drag and drugs, the whole thing. It was a raucous, acidic pantomime version of *Tartuffe*. We'd done previews and we knew the show was working but the end wasn't right. After three hours of this crazy Aussie Christmas where everything went wrong, we hadn't got the last two minutes right. I had cast Lola Nixon, a fabulous vaudeville cabaret musical performer who had been in the Tivoli circuit in the 50s, in the role of the nurse, a character I invented, and she didn't speak for the whole show. That was the whole joke. She was a bit like Barry Humphries's Madge. She didn't speak for three hours, she just watched all the antics, and I thought that maybe Lola needs to say something at the end. And Wayne Harrison, the STC's artistic director, said, and to this day I'll always be grateful for this: 'Oh, I know the line. Try this out at the preview tonight.' It was the last line of the show and then there was blackout. So, after three hours, there was an empty stage and Lola turned around to the audience and in the most fabulous Aussie vaudeville voice, she said: 'Best fuckin' Christmas I've ever had.' To this day, never have I heard an audience roar with laughter at a blackout line like that in the Opera House. It worked and we did it for the rest of the six weeks.

So, I remember the sound of laughter at the Opera House as much as the sound of booing. I have these extremes. There are many, many more stories, but if someone mentions the building to me, I think of Joan Sutherland with a bag of chips by the billiard table, Lola Nixon bringing the show down and the *Nabucco* with the booing and the Whitlams. Whenever I go to the Opera House, I expect to see the Whitlams in the lift, Joan Sutherland by the billiard table, or Lola, God bless her, who's gone up to the great theatre in the sky, as they all have.

— Barrie Kosky is one of the world's most sought-after directors. He has confounded and delighted audiences across Australia, America and Europe, where he spent ten years as intendant of the Komische Oper Berlin. Born in Melbourne, he was artistic director of the Adelaide Festival and co-artistic director of the Vienna Schauspielhaus and has directed multiple productions at the Sydney Opera House.

Following spread_ A scene from Sydney Theatre Company's *Tartuffe*, by Moliere, 1997, directed by Barrie Kosky, in the Drama Theatre. Photo: Tracey Schramm. Courtesy of Sydney Theatre Company.

KATE MULVANY

In January 2015, my play *Masquerade* was performed for the Sydney Festival in the Opera House Drama Theatre. The play was based on *Masquerade*, the best-selling children's book by English author Kit Williams. It told the story of the Moon falling in love with the Sun. In the book, the Moon crafts an amulet from all the gemstones in the world and gives it to her pet hare Jack to deliver to the Sun. But Jack loses the amulet and the reader has to work out where Jack lost it. In addition to writing the book, Kit Williams actually made an amulet of gold and stones that he buried secretly somewhere in the world and put the answers to where it was buried in a coded message in the book. This set off a worldwide treasure hunt.

The book had been given to me when I was in hospital with childhood cancer, and the dream of finding that jewel helped me in my recovery. To have Kit Williams himself entrust me with his celestial love story decades later, and to tell it at the magical Opera House for Griffin Theatre Company and the Sydney Festival, was huge. It was my debut as a playwright at the House, after performing in several shows there over the years, so it was an incredible milestone.

In a stroke of wonder, Kit Williams arranged for the actual *Masquerade* jewel – long since found and owned by an anonymous collector – to be flown from overseas and put on display in the Paspaley store in the Sydney CBD. Paspaley also kindly offered me one of their

Nathan O'Keefe in a scene from *Masquerade* during Sydney
Festival in the Drama Theatre, 2015. Photo: Brett Boardman.

beautiful jewels to wear to the opening of *Masquerade*: a huge pearl encased in a silver mesh lavalier. It was stunning. And it was worth tens of thousands of dollars. I was terrified and awestruck to wear it, especially after the amount of paperwork I signed promising to take diligent care of the jewel.

On the night of the opening, I put on a nice frock, placed the pearl amulet around my neck and made my way to the Opera House. It was a beautiful day. The show was for children and adults, so families were frolicking on the Forecourt as the sun began to set behind the Harbour Bridge. I entered the backstage door and went about dropping off thank you cards and gifts to the cast who were all having an afternoon nap in their dressing rooms after a big week of tech, dress runs and previews. I slid the cards under their doors and left more in the Drama Theatre kitchen for our amazing crew who were still working diligently onstage to get the show ready.

With thirty minutes before the most important performance of my playwriting career, I went outside through the front foyer, sat with my seven-year-old niece, Maisie, and had a champagne handed to me by my husband Hamish. Just as I was about to calm my opening night jitters with a sip, Hamish said, 'Kate … where's the pearl?'

I looked down to the lavalier to see a sad, limp chain, and no pearl where there definitely should have been one. Somewhere in the Opera House I had lost a priceless jewel. Just like Jack Hare.

Quivering with fear, I called out to the ushers –'Hold the show!' – as I wildly retraced my steps, half running, half crawling along the floor. Nothing at Stage Door. Nothing in the concrete corridor to the Drama Theatre, nothing amid the bedazzled opera props that loomed along the walls. Nothing in the backstage bathrooms, or the Drama Theatre kitchen with its Beroccas and Family Assorted biscuits. I ran onto the stage to find actors in full make-up and costumes doing their vocal warm-ups and exercises. 'The jewel! I've lost the jewel!' They laughed, of course, because that's exactly what Jack cries in my just-about-to-open play. But one look at my panic-stricken face and the flaccid chain around my neck and they realised. Our show just got super meta.

At the five-minute call, there were ten fully costumed actors, six crew members, several ushers, a horrified playwright and her niece and husband all crawling around the stage, backstage, every nook and cranny trying to find the bloody pearl. It was the proverbial needle in a haystack. As I clamoured across the seating bank, I noticed a clasp on the chain that had been clearly meant to protect the pearl. Unfortunately, I hadn't noticed it before, and now I owed thousands of dollars to Paspaley. I could practically hear any royalties going down the gurgler.

Suddenly, a voice from our NIDA secondment, Jen: 'I think I found it!'

We rushed to find her. She was standing in Helen Dallimore's dressing room. And there was the pearl. Sitting in the corner of the room. It had fallen from its chain and rolled under the door as I'd shoved Helen's opening night card through.

A miracle, two minutes before showtime.

I wept at Jen's feet with gratitude, apologised to the cast and crew, made my way back to the front of house, and joined the audience as the doors opened to my play. I remember looking at the setting Sun and hoping he knew how much effort had gone into getting his jewel to him. That pearl didn't leave my clutched, sweaty hand all night. Not even for a glass of champagne. And the show was a hit.

I can now hand-on-my-heart say that I know every square metre of the Drama Theatre and its backstage area. Especially the floor.

__ Kate Mulvany OAM is an award-winning playwright, actor and screenwriter.

TIM MINCHIN

... the risk of poverty and obscurity is perceived by many to be worth it, because if you win, there's an asymmetric upside ...

The idea of an asymmetric upside was first introduced to me by radical arty-man David Walsh, daring daddy of Tasmania's iconic MONA, during dinner. The term neatly describes a type of gamble taken where the gambler perceives that the scale of the potential reward is great enough to justify what might initially seem an unacceptable risk.

The asymmetric upside is why you choose to be an artist, though I don't suppose most artists would describe it as that. The risk is high: most artists are poor and many are very unhappy. They are expected to soak up rejection, criticism and derision, all the while maintaining a magical thing called 'self-belief', even though it's likely that the reason you became an artist is because you discovered early that the admiration of others was the only way you could feel any belief at all.

But the risk of poverty and obscurity is perceived by many to be worth it, because if you win, there's an asymmetric upside: you get to manifest your true self, change people's lives, be admired and live forever. Or something like that.

Jørn Utzon's Opera House design was radical. It pushed engineers and politicians, builders and bureaucrats to their limits. In order to achieve its vaulted heights, it required them to dig deep: deep under the harbour floor, deep into their reserves of expertise and faith, and deep into their pockets.

And like all great art, it challenged its audience. It didn't look like anything they'd seen before. It took fucking ages to build. It sucked up taxpayer dollars. It was sneered at by philistines and very nearly undone by political pettiness. It absorbed rejection, criticism and derision. It was completed ten years late and 1357 per cent over budget.

It takes extraordinary talent, tenacity and gonads of steel to make something as timelessly beautiful, as iconic as the Sydney Opera House. The gamble was mind-blowing – but the potential upside was mind-blowinger.

It is always difficult to make the decision to invest in art, because it's so hard to measure the good it does. And it's hard to measure the good it does because the good it does is immeasurable. Especially when the ideas are bold and the risk monumental.

Following spread_ Tim Minchin on the Opera House Forecourt in November 2022. Photo: Damian Bennett.

In my relatively un-monumental career, I have nevertheless at times had to dig deep. Very often in the decade before I cracked it, I nearly gave up. Oftentimes the potential upside didn't seem worth the pain. And in the last decade and a half, since my career took off, I've copped more than my share of fair and unfair derision, of criticism and rejection.

But, my god, has it been worth it. I never dreamed of this upside. Never dreamed I'd get to work with the people I've worked with, to make what I've helped make. I never dreamed of living where I've lived. And I never dreamed I'd play the places I've played. I've performed at Wembley and The O2 and the Royal Albert Hall. I've worked in New York and Hollywood, Dubrovnik and Budapest. South Hedland. Slough.

But, honestly, the Sydney Opera House: there is nothing like her on earth.

I've performed with the Sydney Symphony in her cavernous Concert Hall and sung solo in the Studio, deep in her belly. And like every artist before me and since, I've been lost in the halls of her labyrinthine undercarriage, peering through miserly windows, using the Harbour Bridge as a guiding star, trying to find a loo or my manager or the stage. I've counted down to New Year, begging the producers for a beer, singing clichés, watching garish fireworks reflected in her glass.

But if I had to pick one gig, there's nothing quite like playing the Opera House Forecourt. Sitting at a piano, surrounded by my band, singing in harmony, looking up over thousands of silhouetted Sydney heads, back at those stunning, soaring arches.

Revelling in her asymmetric upside.

— Writer, actor, pianist, singer, composer-lyricist, comedian and producer ... Tim Minchin is one of our most prolific and expansive creatives. From hugely popular live tours to composing hit West End/Broadway musicals *Matilda* and *Groundhog Day*; from writing and starring in award-winning TV series *Upright* to producing an acclaimed studio album, 2020's *Apart Together*, the West Australian multi-hyphenate has taken his talents to the world.

It is always difficult
to make the decision
to invest in art, because
it's so hard to measure
the good it does.

Acknowledgements

A standing ovation to the fifty individuals who so generously and enthusiastically shared their stories for this publication. Their affection for the Sydney Opera House is manifest on every page, reinforcing the value of a building that stands apart not just as an architectural masterpiece but as a personal space full of memories and connections over so many years. Our gratitude to the managers, agents, publicists and assistants whose help behind the scenes has been invaluable throughout the life of this project. Thanks also to Louise Herron and the wider Opera House family, including Ebony Bott, Nicola Brandon, Julia Brown, Anthony Carthew, Brigid Collaery, Lois Farfus, Jessica Gooch, Alethea Giles, Casey Green, Hannah Hibbert, Beau James, Hugh Lamberton, Ben Marshall, Laura Matarese, Jade McKellar, Mathew Millay, Grace Mulders, Nicola Rhind, Natalie Richards, Chip Rolley, Jordana Rowley, Crispin Rice, Janelle Ryan, Weiyi Shi, Carolyn Stewart-Smith, Tessa Pelle and Fiona Winning. A special shout-out to the wonderful folk at the Opera House's resident companies, past and present, including Caitlin Benetatos, Donna Cusack-Muller, Helene Fox, Janet Glover, Judith Seef and Ruth Thomas, and to the New York Philharmonic and Sydney Festival. Thanks also to Andrew McMillen, Zoe Sadokierski, Liza-Mare Syron and Matthew Westwood, and to the Thames and Hudson team, in particular Sally Heath, Alice Marks and Melissa-Jane Fogarty, and designers. Finally, we acknowledge Dr Eileen Ong for her generous support of this project, and thank her for ensuring these stories will endure long into the future.

Credits

First published in Australia in 2023
by Thames & Hudson Australia Pty Ltd
11 Central Boulevard
Portside Business Park
Port Melbourne, Victoria 3207
ABN: 72 004 751 964

thameshudson.com.au

Readers are advised that this book contains
the names and images of people who have
passed away.

Thames & Hudson Australia wishes
to acknowledge that Aboriginal and
Torres Strait Islander people are the first
storytellers of this nation and the traditional
custodians of the land on which we live and
work. We acknowledge their continuing
culture and pay respect to Elders past,
present and future.

ISBN 978-1-760-76389-3 (hardback)
ISBN 978-1-760-76390-9 (ebook)

 A catalogue record for this
book is available from the
National Library of Australia

Every effort has been made to trace
accurate ownership of copyrighted text and
visual materials used in this book. Errors or
omissions will be corrected in subsequent
editions, provided notification is sent to
the publisher.

Design: Pfisterer + Freeman
Editing: Melissa-Jane Fogarty
Proudly printed and bound by Ellikon Fine
Printers, Melbourne, Australia, to ISO14001
Environmental Management Standards
on FSC certified paper.

Paul Kelly Simone Young L
Briggs Clementine Ford Iv
Kitty Flanagan Brian Thon
David McAllister Casey D
Frances Rings Carlotta Re
Paul Nunnari Jennie Begg
Rhoda Roberts Jimmy Ba
Sarah Blasko Deborah Ma
Peter Gilmore Maina Giel
Nikki Gemmell Jordi Sava
Wendy Martin Louis Nowr
Bill Henson Elena Kats-Ch
Graeme Murphy Marcia H
Ngaiire Wendy Blacklock
Lindy Hume Barrie Kosky